365
26
G14

·7·DAY

University of Plymouth
Charles Seale Hayne Library
Subject to status this item may be renewed
via your Primo account

http://primo.plymouth.ac.uk
Tel: (01752) 588588

CCTV

Edited by
Martin Gill

Perpetuity Press

First published 2003
by Perpetuity Press Ltd
PO Box 376 Leicester LE2 1UP
Telephone: +44 (0) 116 221 7778
Fax: +44 (0) 116 221 7171
Email: info@perpetuitypress.com
Website: www.perpetuitypress.com

The information contained in this book is believed to be correct; however, it should
not be treated as a substitute for advice in individual situations. No responsibility for loss
occasioned to any person acting or refraining from action as a result of any statement in
it can be accepted by the authors, editor or publisher.

Chapter 4 is adapted from Scarman Centre National CCTV Evaluation Team (2003)
National evaluation of CCTV early findings on scheme implementation-effective practice
guide. Home Office Development and Practice Report 7. London: Home Office (which
is © Crown copyright 2003). Reproduced with permission of the Home Office.

ISBN 1 899287 71 X

Perpetuity Press

Contents

Acknowledgements

I would like to thank all the contributors to this book for their papers. CCTV is a much discussed subject but there is still very little research on the topic. I am pleased to be able to include a diverse range of papers that cover some pressing issues which have so far received very little attention. I had to badger some of them to deliver more quickly than they wanted (I am not going to say who)—I hope that they will think it was worth it. I would also like to thank the referees who looked at the chapters and offered guidance; their role is an anonymous one and I appreciate their efforts.

I have been greatly encouraged in my work on CCTV by a range of people. Nick Tilley, David Farrington, Kate Painter, Jason Ditton, Mike McCahill and Clive Norris all influenced my thinking in different ways, as have Gwendolyn Brandon, Nicola Douglas, Peter Fry, Chris Kershaw, Tom Levesley, Amanda Martin and Ian Short. Thanks to Sara Millington-Hore for bringing this book together quickly. My colleagues at Perpetuity Research and Consultancy International (PRCI) and the CCTV researchers at the Scarman Centre, University of Leicester were and are a constant source of encouragement. Finally a special thanks to Karen, Emily, Karis and Oliver. Nevertheless, all errors are exclusively my responsibility.

We have a lot to learn about CCTV. There are still those making claims about its effectiveness, or conversely are critical of it in ways that are not always justified by the available independent evidence. It is hoped that this book may move the debate along just a little further by providing some new research findings and a few new ideas.

Martin Gill
June 2003

Contributors

Jenna Allen is currently working for the Scarman Centre as a research assistant on a Home Office sponsored evaluation of CCTV. Her academic background includes a BSc in Human Psychology from Loughborough University, where she specialized in the study of sleep patterns in athletes. She then completed an MSc in Criminology and Criminal Justice, also from Loughborough University, where she conducted a Leicestershire Constabulary sponsored evaluation of CCTV in Ashby-de-la-Zouch. Other areas of interest include crime prevention, policing and community safety.

Javier Argomaniz joined the Scarman Centre's CCTV evaluation project as a social statistician. His previous data analysis work experience includes working as a consultant for SPSS Ireland. His academic background consists of a BSc in Sociology at Universidad del Pais Vasco (Spain); an MSc in Applied Social Research at Trinity College, Dublin, which included a dissertation on modern trends in long-term youth unemployment in Ireland; and an ongoing MA in International Security Studies. His main research interests are the implementation of quantitative research methods in social research, the application of advanced statistical models to the analysis of crime and the implications of transnational crime networks on international security.

Professor David Bull is a founder and currently chairman of ProVision Communication Technologies Ltd, a wireless multimedia spin-off from the University of Bristol. He is also Professor of Signal Processing at the University of Bristol and Head of the Electrical and Electronic Engineering Department where he leads the Signal Processing Research Group. He has worked widely in signal processing with recent research focusing on the problems of image and video communications (in particular error-resilient source coding, linear and non-linear filterbanks, scalable methods, content-based coding and architectural optimization). He has published over 250 papers and two books in these areas and has been awarded two IEE Premiums. He has also been a director of the VCE in Digital Broadcasting and Multimedia Technology and a member of the UK Foresight ITEC panel. He is currently a member of the Science and Technology Board for the UK MoD Defence Technology Centre in Data and Information Fusion and of the DTI-funded research centre 3CRL.

David P. Farrington is Professor of Psychological Criminology at the Institute of Criminology, University of Cambridge. He has published 29 books and monographs and about 300 papers on criminological and psychological topics.

He is director of the Cambridge Study in Delinquent Development and co-investigator on the Pittsburgh Youth Study. He is also chair of the Campbell Collaboration Crime and Justice Coordinating Group, and is a former president of the American Society of Criminology, the British Society of Criminology and the European Association of Psychology and Law.

Sander Flight has studied political science and research methods at the University of Amsterdam. He started his career as a researcher conducting nationwide surveys into crime and safety (cf. Crime Victim Survey). After five years, he switched to DSP-groep where he has been working for nearly three years as a senior researcher in the field of crime prevention. In his recent work, Sander focuses on evaluation projects on CCTV, juvenile delinquency, school safety and Communities that Care.

Matt Follett was a postgraduate student in criminology at the University of Leicester during the years 1997–99 and also a Community Safety Officer and Partnership Development Officer for Leicestershire Constabulary, working with the Leicester Crime and Disorder Partnership. Following work abroad he returned in January 2002 to the University of Leicester to begin on a Home Office funded CCTV evaluation project, carried out by the Scarman Centre. He is currently doing his PhD in the Social Policy and Criminology Department of the Open University in Milton Keynes on the subject of Crime Reduction Partnerships and their role in local governance.

Martin Gill is Director of Perpetuity Research and Consultancy International (PRCI) and a Professor of Criminology at the Scarman Centre, University of Leicester. He has published work on crime, security and policing including over 50 journal and magazine articles and 10 books including *Commercial Robbery* (Blackstone Press*)* and *Managing Security* (Perpetuity Press)*.* He has been involved in a range of projects involving business crime including shop theft, frauds, staff dishonesty, burglary reduction, robbery, the effectiveness of security measures, fraud, money laundering, policing and violence at work. He is currently managing several evaluations of the effectiveness of CCTV including the major national project sponsored by the Home Office. Professor Gill is co-editor of the *Security Journal*.

Patricia Jessiman is currently working for the Scarman Centre as a research assistant on a Home Office sponsored evaluation of CCTV. She has also worked on an ESRC-funded project on the 'Verbal Overshadowing Effect'. Her academic background includes an MA in Psychology from Aberdeen University and an MSc in Psychological Research Methods from Exeter University. She has a particular interest in Forensic Psychology, particularly concerning young offenders.

Deena Kara is currently working for the Scarman Centre as a research assistant on a Home Office evaluation of CCTV. Her academic background is an LL B (Hons) in Law. She then completed an MA in Criminology, where she conducted a study examining police and multi-agency responses to South Asian women experiencing domestic violence in the London Borough of Newham. Other areas of interest include alcohol-related crime and disorder and crime and disorder partnership working.

Johannes Knutsson is Director of Research and Professor in Criminology at the National Police Academy in Oslo, Norway. He has also a part-time position at the Swedish Police Academy. He has published several evaluation studies of crime preventive measures as well as studies on policing, and has just been the editor of a book on Problem-Oriented Policing. Currently he is conducting a comparative study on police use of firearms in Scandinavia.

Ross Little is currently working for the Scarman Centre as a research assistant on a Home Office sponsored evaluation of CCTV. He has also worked on an earlier Crime Reduction Programme project as a part of a multi-disciplinary team evaluating the impact of Burglary Reduction Initiatives. His research background consists of an MA in Criminology at the University of Leicester, preceded by a BSc in Psychology at Sheffield University. Empirical work at the latter included a dissertation on dyslexia and Attention Deficit Disorder (ADD) in a sample of young offenders, while his MA dissertation focused on bail decision-making in one police force. Other areas of interest include eyewitness testimony and the role of juries in sentencing decisions.

Karryn Loveday has a BSc (Hons) in Sociology and Social Research and is undertaking an MSc in Social Research. Following several years as a researcher at the Scarman Centre, University of Leicester, working with Professor Martin Gill, she is now the Crime and Disorder Officer for the Safer Middlesbrough Partnership. She has worked with Professor Gill on a range of projects, including what CCTV operators do and why, evaluations of crime initiatives and patterns and trends in bank robberies, and offenders' perspectives on situational crime prevention measures dealing with the proceeds of their crimes.

Michael McCahill is currently a full-time researcher at the Centre for Criminology and Criminal Justice, University of Hull. His main interests lie in the areas of surveillance and sociological theory, and he has contributed chapters to a number of books in these fields. His most recent work is *The Surveillance Web: The Rise of Visual Surveillance in an English City* (2002, Willan). He is currently working as the UK Research Officer on a comparative study of CCTV surveillance in seven European capital cities entitled UrbanEye. He is a member of the British Society of Criminology and the British Sociological Association.

David Mackay is a recognized authority on the management of town-centre CCTV systems and established the UK's first British Standard CCTV control room. He is a former officer in the Parachute Regiment and was a member of the UK CCTV User Group Standards Committee and also project manager of the Glasgow CityWatch CCTV system for two years. He helped to develop the original CCTV Operator national training standard, and was the CCTV adviser to the National Retail Theft Initiative. He is a security press journalist and has written more than 100 articles. He is a Fellow of the Institute of Supervisory Management and holds degrees in education and security management, and is a Research Associate of the Scottish Centre for Criminology.

Clive Norris is Professor of Sociology in the Department of Sociological Studies at the University of Sheffield. He has written extensively on the sociology of policing, and the sociology of surveillance. His most recent books are *Introducing Criminology,* written with Clive Coleman, and he is joint author of *The Maximum Surveillance Society: The Rise of CCTV* with Gary Armstrong. He is one of the founding editors of a free on-line journal *Surveillance & Society,* and is currently writing a book, provisionally entitled *Crime, Deviance and Surveillance,* to be published in 2005.

Kate A. Painter is Senior Research Associate at the Institute of Criminology, University of Cambridge. She pioneered research in the areas of marital rape and street lighting and crime reduction. Her special areas of expertise include evaluative methods and analysis, survey methods of investigation, gender and crime and victims and the Criminal Justice System. She was Project Manager for the Evaluation of Military Corrective Training on Young Offenders for the Home Office Prison Department. She has wide research experience and has published extensively. Her latest publication is a report for the Home Office on Gender Differences in Risk Factors of Offending, with Professor David Farrington. She was Programme Director of CCTV and Vehicle Crime Reduction, Home Office (2000–1).

Polly Smith has an MSc in Criminology from the University of Leicester and has several years' experience in crime research. She is currently carrying out freelance work in the field of crime prevention and security management. Previous posts include that of Project Manager of a research team conducting an evaluation of CCTV and Research Assistant evaluating the impact of the Reduction of Burglary Initiative. Her research interests include crime prevention and public attitudes towards the control of disorder and anti-social behaviour and the use of CCTV.

Angela Spriggs is Project Manager of a national evaluation of CCTV at the Scarman Centre, University of Leicester. She has wide experience of research in policy, crime and socio-legal institutions. Previous research includes a Home

Office evaluation of Burglary Reduction Initiatives. Her background is in law and psychology.

Daniel Swain is currently working for the Scarman Centre as a research assistant on a Home Office sponsored evaluation of CCTV. His academic background includes an MA in Psychology from Glasgow University and an MSc in Forensic Behavioural Science from Liverpool University. His research interests include the study of 'football crowd disturbances' and forensic psychology.

Yvonne van Heerwaarden has studied Trans-cultural Pedagogics at the University of Groningen. Her final thesis was on gender issues in low-caste families in India. In addition, she published a research paper on domestic violence towards Turkish women. Before she joined DSP-groep she was employed as a freelance researcher at several other agencies. She is now working for DSP-groep at the department of crime prevention. Her main topics are juvenile delinquency, alternative punitive sanctions and domestic violence. She also works extensively with the Child Welfare Council.

Paul van Soomeren has studied urban planning/demography and social geography at the University of Amsterdam. He is one of the founders and directors of the board of the private research and consultancy bureau DSP-groep in Amsterdam (www.dsp-groep.nl). Paul van Soomeren is one of the world leading experts in Crime Prevention Through Environmental Design (CPTED), director of the board of the International CPTED Association (ICA) and president of the European Designing Out Crime Association (www.e-doca.net). He lectures at international workshops and conferences in major fun cities such as Barcelona, Orlando, Brisbane, Stockholm, Sydney, London, Tokyo and Amsterdam.

Brandon C. Welsh is an Assistant Professor in the Department of Criminal Justice at the University of Massachusetts Lowell. His research interests include the prevention of delinquency and crime and economic analysis of prevention and intervention programmes. He is an author and editor of three books, including *Evidence-Based Crime Prevention* with Lawrence Sherman, David Farrington and Doris MacKenzie (Routledge, 2002), and served as an editor of a special issue of the *Annals of the American Academy of Political and Social Science* titled 'What Works in Preventing Crime: Systematic Reviews of Experimental and Quasi-Experimental Research' (2001). Recent articles have appeared in *Justice Quarterly*, *Criminology and Public Policy*, *Crime and Justice: A Review of Research* and *British Journal of Criminology*. He received his PhD in Criminology from the University of Cambridge.

Chris A. Williams is a Research Fellow in the European Centre for the Study of Policing, in the History Department of the Open University. He has published work on the history of policing in the UK, police reform and nineteenth-century urban history, the analysis and deployment of criminal statistics, and the decline in autonomy of urban police forces in the twentieth century. His current research concerns the policing of violence in the UK after 1945, the growth of compensation for criminal injuries, and the nature and extent of links between colonial and 'home' police in the nineteenth and twentieth centuries.

Stig Winge is presently an Adviser at the National Police Directorate in Norway. His main tasks are analysis, crime prevention and implementing problem-oriented policing.

Chapter 1

Introduction

Martin Gill [1]

Closed circuit television cameras (CCTV) are now commonplace across the UK. Indeed, this country has placed enormous faith in CCTV.[2] The Government's Crime Reduction Programme CCTV Initiative committed £170 million to 680 schemes—and this does not include some matched funding from local authorities that amounts to another £40 million, nor money that has been made available from other parts of the government at national and local levels over time. In addition to public space CCTV, cameras are now commonplace in a range of working environments.

Yet paralleling the widespread use of CCTV have been growing doubts about its capacity to deliver on early promises of effectiveness. One recent review of previous evaluation studies has seriously questioned its value.[3] This piece of research has attracted a lot of attention but it potentially understates the positive contribution that CCTV can make. Although very scholarly, the review took no account of a range of important factors,[4] including the level of resources committed to the schemes, the quality of design, the scale of 'buy-in' from stakeholders, the ability of operators and the quality of their training (and whether they were trained at all), the effectiveness of management systems, or the relationship with the police which is a really crucial condition for effectiveness of public schemes. In any event there is potentially much more to effectiveness than whether there is a reduction in crime and whether the public feel safer. CCTV can also be an aid to police investigations, picking up images from different locations to build up an understanding of an offender's routines before and after an offence,[5] or by jogging people's memories, or encouraging offenders to plead guilty where the picture quality is good, enforcing parking and traffic regulations,[6] managing crowds and helping to protect the vulnerable,[7] to name but a few. Although it is possible to point to some obvious successes—for example where images have helped identify offenders—it has yet to be proven that the benefits outweigh the drawbacks or that CCTV is cost-effective. These factors and others are crucial, and will as far as possible be incorporated into a more detailed Home Office sponsored study currently being undertaken.[8]

But concerns about CCTV are not just about its effectiveness[9] and it is worth rehearsing, albeit briefly, some of them here. There is widespread debate about what is the best CCTV technology; this ranges from the relative advantages in investing in analogue and digital systems[10] to the pros and cons of redeployable versus static systems, and the potential for open circuit television cameras (OCTV). Technology is developing fast. It is not easy to keep up, and one of the dangers is that new schemes are used as guinea pigs for technology being tested in demanding environments for the first time. The whole topic of technology probably merits a book in its own right; suffice it to say that there is a need to track the best developments, ensure they are evaluated rigorously and offer more guidance to those at the sharp end about the relative advantages and disadvantages of different types.

It is emerging that the effective use of CCTV will often generate considerable resource implications. There is no doubt that CCTV affords the opportunity of surveilling more areas from remote locations—but noticing something is going on and having the resources to respond are separate matters. Rural areas are a case in point: CCTV offers the opportunity for an isolated area that does not justify a police presence to be surveilled, but, when events are discovered, its very isolation makes a speedy police presence difficult. In due course, and as the public becomes more informed about these limitations, the issues will need to be managed to avoid public disenchantment. Some of the developing uses of CCTV such as number plate recognition systems require significant back-up resources. Even stopping a stolen vehicle can be a problem. As one police officer noted:

> You have to ask, is the driver wanted for something else? Other enquiries then have to be made. If stolen goods are found in the car then this will result in further enquiries. If an arrest is made, is there room at the police station? If not you need to go to another station. If suicidal he or she will need to be watched all the time. Then there is the time it takes for a solicitor or doctor to come—interviewing cannot start without them. Meanwhile the car has to be watched until it is recovered, you might be able to get a traffic warden to help but not always. Then if the person is charged you may have to appear in court the next day so the file has to be written up before leaving the shift so that it can be submitted to the court. Then you will go to the court, but you will rarely give evidence. Meanwhile the number plate recognition system is going off with lots of opportunities which are not exploited. It is frustrating when you stop a car for no vehicle licence when a car with armed robbers goes by.

Indeed, this conundrum illustrates that the need to respond to incidents captured on CCTV is one of its main limitations. It is far from clear that sending a police officer every time would be the best policy, even if were possible. Recently one policy-maker noted in a personal interview that it is better to ignore some incidents, for example youths arguing, in that they invariably ended quickly and that police attendance can often escalate events. This approach needs to be developed to help manage public expectations and it is not yet clear how this is being done.

But not all systems are monitored and of those that are not all of them are monitored all of the time, although it is far from clear that the public realize this. We need to know a lot more about the best ways to monitor scenes, how to identify suspicious behaviour and how to transmit suspicions to those on the front line.[11] This is another area where research is weak and where the implications are unexamined.

There are genuine concerns about the use of CCTV to raise revenue. While the public have generally welcomed CCTV as a crime prevention and community safety tool, there are genuine concerns about it being used a revenue generator. This is most visibly apparent in the widespread use of roadside cameras which are used to catch speeding motorists. In fact there are a number of examples of CCTV being used to generate income, for example from increased housing rents or direct from businesses. In one Dutch town centre there are big screens so that people can see themselves being watched and they also provide an advertising opportunity. There is certainly more mileage in this issue yet and it is likely to engender strong reactions, firstly from those who are being asked to pay (and not just via speeding fines) and secondly from those providing the services, who are looking for what they may view as essential revenue.

There is also concern that many CCTV systems are not complying with the law.[12] This is accompanied by confusion about the management of data subject requests, where people have a right to see any pictures taken of them. There are many potentially costly problems that have yet to be understood, particularly if large numbers of people request images at the same time. Then there is the concern that people may eventually begin to resent the 'big brother' effect,[13] or lots of 'little brothers',[14] especially if they begin to doubt its effectiveness. Already some operators are disillusioned about what they see as the lack of police interest in their work and the lack of feedback on the success of police operations in which they are involved. These are merely examples of concerns that exist, but they are ones that need to be monitored, evaluated and managed.

The purpose of this book is to provide some answers to some of the questions that have been raised by incorporating the latest research findings in the area. As noted, there is not a great deal of research on emerging issues, and what there is needs updating. The following chapters provide new insights into how funding for CCTV is won by local authorities, put forward fresh evidence on the extent and legality of CCTV, incorporate a European dimension with papers from the Netherlands and Norway, and discuss issues which have received little attention in the past, such as offenders' views, displacement and the promise of technology.

In Chapter 2 Chris Williams traces the history of CCTV, and it has a longer past than some may have assumed. Williams argues that the use of CCTV continued a process of centralization and mechanization of the police that began in the 1930s. Initially police experiments in using CCTV in London for crowd control were unsuccessful. They were followed by schemes in Liverpool and London directed against street crime. The Home Office concluded that these had a limited impact and were hard to evaluate, although the forces concerned were keen to play up their role as a deterrent. Williams argues that many of the features of the 'new surveillance' were in fact present in the surveillance systems of the 1960s, thus calling into question any easy association between this phenomenon and post-industrial society.

Chapter 3 is the first of two chapters that look at implementation issues. David Mackay assesses via a case study what factors influence the introduction of and support for CCTV. He concludes that the availability of central government funding is the overriding reason. Supporting explanations include the fact that CCTV is championed for its perceived positive effect on the local economy; that there is a need to be seen to be 'doing something' about crime; that there is a concern that the lack of town centre CCTV generates a 'second-class' image; and that it is seen as a management tool and, indeed, very seldom as a crime prevention measure.

In Chapter 4 some of the same conclusions are reached, albeit by a different methodology. Smith *et al.* also found that money is not always given to the most needy, and identified that, on occasions, those that shout loudest obtain grants. This chapter discusses some of the practical problems in submitting bids for funding and then in implementing a CCTV scheme. There is nothing new in the finding that difficulties occur in partnership working, specifically where agreements were not always seen through to conclusion. But one of the more important issues for future funding initiatives is that schemes struggled to collect good data to support a bid. The methodology was sometimes very weak, and not everyone found it easy to follow the Home Office advice available at the time. Schemes need more advice up front in making bids—it is an expert task and this needs to be recognized.

In Chapter 5 Mike McCahill and Clive Norris discuss the extent, sophistication and legality of CCTV, a much under-discussed topic. In their first survey of 27 commercial/civic institutions in the London Borough of Wandsworth they found that half of them had a CCTV system in operation. In their second survey of publicly accessible premises on a busy high street they found that almost half had CCTV systems in operation. By extrapolating the average number of cameras in these institutions, they 'guestimate' that there are more than 4 million surveillance cameras in operation. Only a minority had the required legal signage, thus suggesting that nearly 80 per cent of the CCTV systems in London's business space are not compliant with the Data Protection Act.

The next chapter begins a discussion about an issue that has remained unanswered during the development of CCTV, namely whether it works or not. Chapter 6 discusses the principles of evaluation. David Farrington and Kate Painter note that high-quality research is needed to evaluate the impact of CCTV on crime. They argue that too many past evaluations have been 'quick and dirty'. The authors note that the main criteria of methodological quality are statistical conclusion validity, internal validity, construct validity, external validity and descriptive validity. Their minimum acceptable evaluation design is to have before and after measures of crime in experimental and comparable control areas. They argue that future evaluations should have several experimental and control areas, surveys of potential victims and potential offenders and a long time series of crime rates before and after CCTV. They call for future evaluations to measure displacement and diffusion of benefits by using adjacent and non-adjacent control areas and should test hypotheses about mediators and moderators.

At least a start is made on this in Chapter 7 which discusses offenders' views and in Chapter 8 which investigates displacement. In Chapter 7 Karryn Loveday and I discuss our findings on interviews with street robbers, fraudsters, burglars and shop thieves in prison. They do not worry much about being caught on CCTV, even though some had found camera images used in evidence against them. There is a serious possibility that offenders underestimate the potential threat that CCTV offers. As picture quality improves, operators become more effective and better use is made of the images, so the benefits of CCTV can be used to catch offenders off guard. One striking finding is that those who had been caught on camera in the past were significantly more likely to see CCTV as a threat. Each capture has then this additional advantage.

In Chapter 8 Sander Flight, Yvonne van Heerwaarden and Paul van Soomeren discuss their findings on another much neglected issue, displacement. Their paper is based on an evaluation of three CCTV schemes in Amsterdam. They found that crime decreased and a slight but significant reduction in fear of crime could be observed in one of the three areas. For most crimes and incivilities, there were no indications of displacement in the so-called 'probable displacement area', neither were there signs that fear of crime had been displaced to adjacent areas.

In Chapter 9 Karryn Loveday and I discuss the findings from a project that looked at the effects of CCTV in a retail environment, where some stores had designated CCTV staff and others did not. The evidence suggests that stores with designated CCTV operators generate more benefits to the security of a store. This is reflected in the fact that stores where the CCTV system was monitored by a designated operator benefited from a higher theft discovery rate, together with a higher stock recovery rate. Consequently, this reduced loss and at the same time provided a more accessible focal point for security for all colleagues within the store. Indeed, the research identified that there were opportunities to improve the visibility of a CCTV operator's impact on loss. The key issues are identified as the training and management of the operators and better systems for intelligence sharing between different branches.

In Chapter 10 Stig Winge and Johannes Knutsson discuss an evaluation of CCTV at Oslo Central Railway Station. The findings, as is so often the case with CCTV, offer a mixed message. They show a significant increase in recorded incidents in the area covered by CCTV, indicating an increased detection rate, partly, the authors suggest, because of the CCTV scheme and partly by more police officers patrolling the area. Improvements were noted by locals but, overall, the evaluation could not document any direct effects on criminality, public order or feelings of safety. In Norway at least, the jury is still out.

The final chapter examines technology issues. David Bull argues that in the future technology can provide new methods of support for the acquisition, manipulation and communication of high-quality video data. The emergence of advanced communications technology, such as broadband wireless LANs, will facilitate more rapid and flexible deployment of CCTV systems. Bull notes that high quality coverage will be enabled through the use of IP networks, both wired and wireless, with enhanced performance being obtained through optimization of both video quality and communications performance. Event analysis of video material will be greatly improved through the use of data fusion and other techniques, thus leading to improved operations management. The future, in theory at least, looks good.

Since it arrived on the scene CCTV has attracted many advocates and some critics. More information is needed about its value in different circumstances and about the best ways of managing its potential to be effective, including a greater understanding of other measures it can work with to produce outcomes and the length of time any effect may last.[15] To the neutral the jury is still out, but the collective evidence in this book suggests some room for optimism and some cautious words too, including some scepticism. Hopefully this book will move this process forward in some small way by providing a more informed basis for thinking strategically about CCTV, but there is still a lot more work to be done.

Notes

1   Professor Martin Gill is Director of Perpetuity Research and Consultancy International (PRCI) Ltd and a Professor of Criminology at the University of Leicester; email: m.gill@perpetuitygroup.com. He is grateful to D. Mackay for comments on an earlier draft of this chapter.

2   Some argue that the level of public acceptance is overstated. For example see, Ditton, J. (2000) Crime and the City: Public Attitudes Towards Open-Street CCTV in Glasgow, *British Journal of Criminology*, Vol. 40, No. 4, pp 692–709.

3   Welsh, B.C. and Farrington, D.P. (2002) *Crime Prevention Effects of Closed Circuit Television: A Systematic Review*, Home Office Research Study No. 252. London: Home Office. See also Armitage, R. (2002) *To CCTV or Not? A Review of Current Research into the Effectiveness of CCTV Systems in Reducing Crime*. London: NACRO.

4   Mainly because the original authors of studies failed to provide this information.

5   Gerrard, G. (2002) *Silent Witness: The Police View of CCTV's Role in Crime Reduction*. Presentation to Evaluating the Real Evidence on CCTV. 27 November, Leicester.

6   See, for example, *CCTV Image*, February 2003, pp 10–11.

7   As noted by Newburn, T. and Hayman, S. (2002) *Policing, Surveillance, and Social Control: CCTV and Police Monitoring of Suspects*. Willan: Cullompton.

8   A major evaluation is being undertaken by a team of researchers led by the author.

9   For a more detailed discussion of some of the limitations and criticisms of CCTV see contributions to Norris, C., Moran, J. and Armstrong, G. (eds) (1998) *Surveillance, Closed Circuit Television and Social Control*. Aldershot: Ashgate.

10   See, for example, *Security Management Today*, January 2003, p 39.

11   See Chapter 8.

12   See Chapter 4; also see *Security Park*, 30 May 2002. The feature reports on a survey by Macbond Ltd which concluded that up to 90 per cent of CCTV operators may not be complying with the Data Protection Act 1998. Also 'official sounding data protection registration forms' are exploiting this situation for profit—see *Professional Security*, February 2003, p 30.

13   For a good discussion of this issue see, McCahill, M. (2002) *The Surveillance Web: The Rise of Visual Surveillance in an English City*. Willan: Cullompton.

14   Graham, S. (1998) *Towards the Fifth Utility?* In Norris et al., op. cit.

15   For a discussion about this issue see contributions to Painter, K. and Tilley, N. (eds) (1999) *Surveillance of Public Space: CCTV, Street Lighting and Crime Prevention*, Crime Prevention Studies, Vol. 10. Monsey NY: Criminal Justice Press.

Chapter 2

Police Surveillance and the Emergence of CCTV in the 1960s

Chris A. Williams[1]

Although most commentators have dated their arrival to the 1980s, the use of public CCTV systems by the British police has a history that stretches back 40 years. Initial experiments in the 1960s with CCTV in London and Liverpool were unsuccessful due to the high cost of cabling. The first permanent use was the surveillance of political demonstrations in central London. This fitted into existing police operational requirements and structures, and continued a process of centralization and mechanization that began in the 1930s with working practices originally deployed in the First World War. The arrival of police surveillance systems in the 1960s thus calls into question any easy theoretical association between them and 'post-industrial society'.

'By this means, the necessity of sending out emissaries to reconnoitre the conduct of the lieges would be superseded, since everything would take place, as it were, under the eyes of the police.' Comment on the arrest of a pickpocket following observation through Glasgow's *camera obscura*, 1824.[2]

Introduction

The idea of modern policing has always been about omniscience and omnipotence: about knowledge and ability to act. The reality of modern policing (so far) has been the inability of human institutions to attain this ideal. But the idea has a power. The establishment of general visual surveillance in public places can be normative even when it is not sophisticated enough to be instrumental, thus it is a key development. This essay will sketch some landmarks in the history of police surveillance in Britain, focusing on one significant component of this concept, the use of closed circuit television, to answer a question posed by David Lyon: 'If this is how things are done today, was it always like this, and what brought about the changes?'[3] It will begin, though, by giving an account of some of the ways that police surveillance operated in the century before the arrival of CCTV. Then it will show how the Metropolitan Police in particular adopted this technology after some years of experiment, in a way that reinforced their existing working practices and their key priorities. Finally, it examines some of the implications of these findings for some theoretical models of CCTV use in modern society.

'Surveillance' is taken here to have three major aspects. It works within an organization such as the police force, as well as being a component of the institution's interaction with the public world. It can have an instrumental component, altering the way that institutions behave; in this case, of course, systems of surveillance need to be coupled with organizational forms designed to support them. On top of this, it can have a symbolic function above and beyond the instrumental one: the feeling of being watched can be more pervasive than the actual system warrants.[4]

The history of police CCTV surveillance of public areas before the mid-1980s appears to have been largely overlooked.[5] There are a few exceptions, notably Manwaring-White, who in 1983 wrote about CCTV use as an expression of the desire by police to find technological solutions to their problems in the 1970s.[6] The abstract of a recent article in *Security Journal* held that CCTV 'has been in use by security and law enforcement for the last three decades'.[7] In fact, it has been in use for over four decades, since the late 1950s. Norris and Armstrong, who explain the explosion in CCTV use from the 1990s in the context of the end of the Cold War, do not appear aware of the police experiments in the 1960s, and date the first 'permanent and systematic use of CCTV outside the private retail sector' to 1975.[8] A look at the reasons why and ways in which the British police attempted to use this technology and the first sustained operational use of this technology will demonstrate that the process of adoption was intimately connected with many of the concerns at the heart of policing in the postwar period.

Surveillance and policing in general

From the development of the concept of the 'New Police' in the late eighteenth century, the beat policeman was designed as, among other things, a machine for surveillance. He was to monitor a defined area, bringing it under his view, and reporting what went on to his superior officers.[9] He was to pay particular attention to the category of people labelled 'rogues and vagabonds': strangers, and those with no visible means of support.[10] General surveillance had to have limits, and one way that these were arrived at was to make it especially applicable to those who were in an ambivalent social position: the people later referred to as 'police property'. From 1857 each police force had to send to the Home Office the number of the following in their area: known thieves and depredators; receivers of stolen goods; prostitutes; suspected persons; vagrants and tramps. Also required of the police were the numbers of houses of bad character and resorts of thieves and prostitutes, the latter subdivided into public houses, beer shops and coffee shops, brothels and houses of ill fame, and tramps' lodging houses.

As the nineteenth century drew on, the specific targets of surveillance changed. The threat was seen as less from the 'outcast class' as a whole, and more from a group of habitual professional criminals existing in a definable underworld, which could be delimited by police surveillance. Weiner has written that 'as prison walls rose up around the now-private punishments of the convicted, the institutions of the state tried to symbolically know and fix the location of the unconvicted felon.'[11] This trend culminated in the 1869 and 1871 Habitual Offenders Acts, which submitted released prisoners to constant police surveillance. These were informed by studying the French system of registration of convicts, which was investigated by the Home Office in the 1850s.[12] In 1897 the Habitual Criminals Registry was moved from the Home Office to the Metropolitan Police ('Met'). It had ceased to be an administrative device and instead began to function as a tool of real-time policing. Each week, every police force in the country was circulated with the details of those convicts judged likely to reoffend who had been released from custody.[13]

Attempts to run the habitual criminals register using the latest in visual technology met with mixed success.[14] Many prison governors, individual police officers and police forces photographed prisoners in a variety of poses in an attempt to build up a coherent and searchable archive capturing the appearance of members of the criminal class. But while this technique had depth, it was essentially analogue rather than digital. It did not produce data that could be reduced to textual or numerical form and thus easily searched and cross-referenced. The Met briefly adopted the French Bertillon system of unique anthropomorphic measurements for identification, but this in turn was succeeded by the system of fingerprinting, pioneered in India by Edward Henry, and brought by him to Britain when he joined the Met in 1901. Visual identification through the photograph was seductive, and in tune with existing detective practice that utilized personal contact, but the technology was unable to articulate itself to the needs of a massive centralized bureaucracy of surveillance—there were over a million fingerprints on file by 1950.[15] Habitual criminals were registered and tracked, while the mass of the population was patrolled and exposed to the normative figure of the policeman on the beat.[16] In the twentieth century, though, the move towards a car-based culture and dispersed suburbs meant that the population became increasingly difficult to monitor.[17] The working classes were still geographically concentrated and largely fixed, but after 1945 even that was to change. Police grappled with new systems of human-based surveillance, such as light motorcycle patrols and the 'unit beat' system immortalized in *Z Cars*. But the demand for surveillance, and the associated crisis in policing, was apparent.

As the advocates of the 'social construction of technology' (SCOT) model have reminded us, social, political and cultural developments are not determined by technology. As Constant put it: 'Larger systems are inevitably sociotechnical and organizational (they have a large "software" component); their pieces are not necessarily mechanically interconnected'.[18] New technology has to fit into an existing organizational framework—although once in place, it does not necessarily leave the organization unchanged. The adoption of CCTV by police in the UK conforms closely to this model in many respects. The centralized and real-time technological control of London's policing predates the arrival of CCTV by several decades. In 1934 the Met under Commissioner Trenchard set up an Area Wireless Scheme, with a complementary information room and map room, to create a real-time operational headquarters, in which the position of radio cars was plotted on maps, and a 'central organization through which suitable information' could be collated and disseminated.[19] By 1936 the number of messages this centre received had grown from 4,500 per month to 7,900, and six men were on duty at all times (five on telephones and one on the wireless) to ensure a prompt response, since 'the very essence of the work of the Information Room is that all messages must be dealt with promptly on receipt.'[20] The telephonists were constables, working under the control of a CID sergeant, who was able to monitor and cut into their conversations with the public and patrols.[21]

The essential elements of the system had a clear origin in military practice. Grid maps, coloured counters moved by plotters, a strict demarcation of tasks, centralization of information and a senior officer able to cut into his subordinates' lines had all been pioneered by the Royal Flying Corps and continued by Trenchard's Royal Air Force in the air defence of London in the First World War.[22] In the absence of the sergeant in charge, the PCs were not trusted to exercise discretion over serious cases, but had to contact the duty inspector before passing on any messages 'involving the arrest or detention of persons'.[23] The Met, therefore, was utilizing its constables not as independent agents, but as cogs in a wheel whose job it was to apply some intelligence, but not too much, to their role. Trenchard himself, indeed, wondered whether or not civilian clerks could be employed in this role, but he became convinced that 'police knowledge' was necessary to perform this task.[24] Real-time centralized control of policing, therefore, is a clear example of the transmission of technology from military to law enforcement.[25] It is an example of what Ericson and Haggerty see as the desire of police forces for 'organization security' via 'their ability to structure knowledge within predictable apparently fact-based formats, and to transmit this knowledge rapidly to members of the organization in various locations.'[26]

The emergence of CCTV as an option

The first recorded police proposal to investigate the operational use of TV—in this case to control the deployment of police officers—came with the royal wedding in 1947. The request from a Met superintendent to 'evaluate' the BBC's coverage was turned down on the grounds of expense.[27] In the late 1950s, police forces (beginning with Durham in 1956) began to use CCTV to assist in the one-man operation of traffic lights.[28] The technical level required for this to work was not great, nor was its impact on existing police practice.

Official encouragement for the police to equip themselves with new and more advanced tools for the job was part of a desire on the part of many senior police officers and Home Office civil servants to utilize police manpower more effectively by the use of technology.[29] Technology in itself was seen as an unalloyed good, as was demonstrated by the comments of a Met detective superintendent in 1961, who

> said that he favoured the use of any new equipment which would be of assistance in the fight against crime, because thieves were availing themselves of technical aids where possible and police could not afford to lag behind. He said that, in spite of this, he could not put forward any really good reasons for introducing the equipment at present.[30]

Desire for technology in the abstract could sit happily with a complete lack of any operational requirement.

In 1960 the Association of Chief Police Officers, already a powerful institution with direct access to the Home Office, sponsored a Police Equipment Exhibition at the national police training college at Ryton-on-Dunsmore, which was opened by the Permanent Secretary from the Home Office.[31] It was this exhibition that prompted the Met to test the state of the art in TV cameras, which were at that time being promoted by their manufacturers in a wide variety of roles.[32] Several officers who were present noted potential applications for CCTV, including transmitting pictures of suspects, traffic control and ceremonial occasions. One superintendent pointed out that a traffic control system of concealed cameras in the House of Commons, Trafalgar Square and Hyde Park area would have the added feature that 'the value of this system when political meetings break out in disorder would prove of immense value and enable reserves to be despatched to the exact seat of the trouble with the minimum of delay.'[33]

Already in 1960 cameras were available with remote pan, tilt and zoom, weatherproof housings and lens wipers. Two were lent to the Met free of charge by EMI and erected in Trafalgar Square to monitor the crowds at the state visit of the Thai royal family in 1960. Later that year they were re-erected, in conjunction with floodlights, to monitor what one assistant commissioner called 'the usual Guy Fawkes rabble' in the Square on November 5th.[34] The first test was foiled by rain and associated glare, the second by inadequate lighting. Senior officers recognized their potential, but decided this was not preferable to the rival option. One policeman wrote that 'in dealing with ceremonials, potentially disorderly meetings and the like I know of no substitute for the experienced police eye on the spot and the ability to sense trouble in the air.'[35] Despite this technical failure, a subsequent meeting of senior Met officers identified a number of areas where CCTV could conceivably aid policing, from catching pickpockets at the Derby to deterring theft from vehicles in the West End, but also concluded that 'an officer with binoculars' could perform most of these tasks as effectively. The only proposals to stand up were from the Special Branch representative present, who thought that cameras could have a role in scanning for trouble-makers on ceremonial occasions, and keeping a 'distant watch' on 'crowded parts of a line-of-route' that were currently monitored by plain-clothes police.[36]

In 1964, Liverpool police experimented with covert CCTV at various locations in their central area. The four cameras used were lent by electronics companies.[37] They were mounted in buildings in the central business district with the cooperation of the owners, and fed images through to a monitor screen in the same building, from which a police officer was in radio contact with special plain-clothes patrols. Writing in *Security Gazette*, the Chief Constable of Liverpool acknowledged that he expected the public to oppose general surveillance of public places unless it was closely linked to fighting crime:

> It was appreciated at the start of the scheme that the introduction of television as a means of crime detection . . . might cause an adverse reaction from the general public if they were not taken into our confidence and assured that there would be no intrusion into their private lives and liberties.[38]

The remedy was 'maximum publicity to underline the reasons for its introduction', and he hailed an 'encouraging' reaction from the public and the press. His report laid great stress on the power of CCTV to stop 'attacks on . . . persons and property'—despite the fact that very few or no crimes of violence were in fact detected by it. The camera operators were in touch with plain-clothes police drawn from a group of 59 assigned to the operation.[39] The publicity was managed to maximize a deterrent effect. The number of cameras and their location was kept secret, up to the point of not mentioning them in court. Before cheap videotape technology, cameras were of little use for gathering evidence directly. Speculation about their use outside the Central Division had 'not been discouraged' by police.

Liverpool police claimed that the cameras had cut crime, but the Home Office's statisticians were deliberately sceptical with Liverpool's results. Their report seems designed to dismiss the claims made for the role of TV in the experiments, and instead offered a more convincing explanation: the swamping of the area with 59 plain-clothes police had reduced certain property crimes at certain times.[40] They also attributed the drop in crime to the publicity: the camera coverage 'was limited both in time, by the light available, in area and also in definition'.[41] By 1969, even the Liverpool police's own view of what they had called 'Operation Commando' was that: 'no arrests were made as a result of television surveillance. The effect was preventative but largely psychological and therefore the camera had to be moved around to be effective.'[42]

The Met then felt obliged to test its own cameras. It tried them out covertly in two locations, in response to specific crime scares: in Hatton Garden against the fencing of stolen property, and in Ruislip against an outbreak of bicycle theft. In both cases, arrests were few, but the deterrent effect was hailed. The report on the Hatton Garden trial, after detailing the three arrests made, claimed that one of the many beneficial effects was that 'many thieves came to notice, and their activities were kept under close surveillance'. Above all, the report noted that the 'legitimate business traders' in the area were delighted with the extra protection of the scheme.[43] In a 1965 report on the technical and planning considerations for subsequent similar operations, the Met's Research and Planning Branch concluded: that pan and tilt cameras were essential; that they should be sited as unobtrusively as possible; and that to be effective the operator needed to be in constant communication with officers with miniature personal radios. One major consideration was efficiency: 'The use of closed-circuit television can only be justified if it produces a saving of manpower as against any other method of achieving the same result'—a conclusion which was extended to point out that the maximum efficiency would therefore be attained through using a large number of cameras operated by one man. A high degree of visual coverage would produce a situation in which 'one pair of officers can satisfactorily cover a large area when provided by the man on the monitor with accurate information as to what is occurring throughout their area.'[44] CCTV, therefore, held out the attraction that the police institution could be better informed and better coordinated in real time: that technology could help the organization integrate a collection of autonomous police officers into a unit that could react as one. So far, the main thrust of the doctrine dealt with detection of theft, but the report's authors noted that if the equipment was purchased, then it could also be used in 'other instances'. In February 1966 the Commander of the Branch wrote that: 'I consider that an even wider field of application can be opened by the use of camera with publicity, and with manpower for enforcement. In effect, this would be a psychological attack upon the criminal'.[45] This was the next step that they tried.

A use for CCTV

In the 1960s, placing cameras was relatively easy: the problem was putting the images into the control room where the senior policemen were. Since the 1930s radio had been used by the Met to control the deployment of police in real time from a central point, both for everyday policing and, using a specially-made mobile transmitting station, for demonstrations.[46] But TV pictures could not be transmitted, and cabling was too expensive for most locations. The General Post Office keenly guarded their monopoly on cable use, and charged £450 for the first mile used to transmit the image, and £300 for the second mile: a further £22 per mile was needed to transmit the control signals to the camera and housing. One user group who had access to their own free cabling was the railways, and in 1965 British Railways installed cameras to cover the track near Dagenham in an attempt to cut vandalism.[47] The Met experiment of 1967/68 was the most ambitious yet, involving four cameras in one area, cabled into the local police station. The total technical cost of this experiment was £7,800, of which £5,500 covered the purchase of equipment and the rest was taken up by the GPO fees for 'cable hire, connection, and transfer of equipment.'[48] It was to run in two areas (Croydon and Chelsea) consecutively, with each area trial beginning in secret and then being given publicity after a few weeks.[49] It ran in Croydon from December 1967 with indifferent success, but was interrupted. In July 1968, the new Commissioner, John Waldron, anxious to avoid a repeat of the disorder at the recent demonstration against the Vietnam War, called a high-level conference on public order. There, plans were made for CCTV coverage of Grosvenor Square and the route of the next demonstration in October.[50] The planned Chelsea experiment was scrapped and the four cameras from Croydon re-erected along the route. Monitors and a video tape machine were installed in Scotland Yard and in the office of the Home Secretary, James Callaghan, at his request. Cameras were being used not merely to monitor the crowd, but to monitor and control the response of the police to it. As Ericson and Haggerty put it: 'The very communication formats and technologies police officers use to conduct surveillance of others are also used for surveillance of their own work.'[51]

After the demonstration, the TV cameras were hailed as a great success, although the Met top brass were disappointed that they had not managed to capture any scenes of disorder on tape. They concluded: 'There is no doubt that these facilities were invaluable to the officer in command and they contributed to the successful outcome of the operation.'[52] The fifty or so observers from the National Council for Civil Liberties who were present on the demonstration do not appear to have noticed the cameras.[53] Three of the temporary sites immediately became permanent. Two more were added in early 1969, with Home Office approval, to improve the coverage of Whitehall and Parliament Square. From then on, TV cameras became a permanent fixture in the most politically sensitive area of London. The first permanent surveillance system covered a geographically limited area and was installed to help defend the heart of the state. Whitehall and the area around Parliament have a special significance for police officers, especially when Parliament is sitting. They form an area which the police have always seen as theirs to control, or theirs to lose. As Waddington found in the early 1990s:

> The police would 'die in a ditch' to maintain access to the Palace [of Westminster]. To allow even this breach of the sessional order risked creating a resignation issue for the Commissioner himself, according to some senior officers involved in the planning [of policing demonstrations].[54]

He also recorded that other traditionally sensitive areas for the Met include foreign embassies, notably the US Embassy in Grosvenor Square. The Met concluded that for demonstrations: 'the value of CCTV ... is beyond question'.[55] In public, though, they claimed that the cameras in central London were all intended for traffic control.[56]

By 1969, 14 different forces were using CCTV: a total of just 67 cameras nationally. Many forces had just one or two, and only four were making use of video recorders in any way.[57] As we have seen, in the 1960s and 1970s technological constraints made any general and total public surveillance prohibitively expensive, owing chiefly to the high cost of transmission, but this did not stop many police officers from desiring it.

The theoretical implications of the historical perspective

This investigation into how the adoption of CCTV technology by the British police actually happened has implications for a number of theoretical interpretations of this development. It certainly adds weight to the argument that technology is socially constrained and constructed by existing institutional forms rather than writing its own outcome on a blank slate.

The CCTV system that was adopted by the Met had to fit into its existing operational practices and institutions, being used as a feature of the existing centralized operations room controlling large public order policing operations. Once there, the new technology allowed for a greater degree of centralization in this control. To this extent it tends to conform to the SCOT model.[58] Other aspects of its use, though, are consistent with what Graham and Marvin describe as the 'political economy' models of the adoption of new technology.[59] This argument—that the adoption of public visual surveillance is driven by the economic and political requirements of consumer capitalism—is also inherent in Sim's study of the eventual adoption of a large-scale CCTV system in

Liverpool.[60] The British police had a number of operational requirements for the use of cameras, but for most of these during the 1960s, the costs were considered too great to make their use worthwhile. The one major exception to this was in the protection of the geographical area that contained the most essential organs of the state. Guaranteeing the inviolability of these was and is a key part of the Met's task—technology in this case was a way of further increasing the physical protection of the executive, and hence its power to ignore popular protest.

McCahill has concluded that public open-space surveillance systems do not tend to produce 'panopticon effects', but nevertheless the police who first introduced these systems in both Liverpool and London were consciously attempting to achieve these effects from a small number of cameras, and played up publicity and rumours accordingly.[61] An examination of the attempts in the 1960s to use CCTV to cut crime tends to support the arguments of Thrift about the defining role of social systems in the adoption of new technologies, which points out contingency and the role of networks rather than the idea of the new in 'splendid isolation'.[62] The presentation of CCTV as a general instrument of surveillance also has theoretical implications dealing with the timing of the demand for surveillance. Gary Marx has defined the concept of 'new surveillance', featuring new technologies that can 'probe more deeply, widely and softly than normal methods'.[63] The police camera installations of the 1960s meet the majority of the criteria that he sets out for it. Just how new, therefore, is the 'new surveillance', originating as it did in a firmly Fordist era?

Conclusion

CCTV fitted into an existing police design to control more tightly the police organization itself, as well as the desire of this organization as a whole to have a greater power of surveillance, which predated its technological maturity. In controlling crime, the instrumental impact of CCTV was not great. Its symbolic impact, on the other hand, as the cause of a general deterrent effect, was seized upon by police officers. In effect it provided an extension of the surveillance offered by the man on the beat. CCTV could also be put to good use in the centralized control of officers engaged in policing demonstrations, especially since the most problematic of these occurred in the limited geographical area suited to the expensive systems of the day. To use the terms defined by Bruno Latour, the Metropolitan Police operations room, supported by CCTV and other data inputs, provided one example of a 'centre of calculation'. These enable 'action at a distance' to be authorized, controlled and monitored, and reduce the complexity of outside developments to 'such a scale that a few men and women can dominate them by sight . . . they all help to reverse the balance of forces between those who master and those who are mastered.'[64]

Notes

1   Chris Williams has published work on: the history of policing in the UK; police reform and nineteenth century urban history; the analysis and deployment of criminal statistics; and the decline in the autonomy of urban police forces in the twentieth century. His current research concerns the policing of violence in the UK after 1945, the growth of compensation for criminal injuries, and the nature and extent of links between colonial and 'home' police in the nineteenth and twentieth centuries. He can be contacted at Arts Faculty, Open University, Milton Keynes, MK7 6AA, chris.williams@open.ac.uk. This paper grew out of an interdisciplinary panel at Essex University on the 'History of State Surveillance and Information Gathering'. Thanks are due to Clive Emsley, Eddy Higgs, Joe Sim, Francis Dodsworth, Phil Agre, Martin Gill, an anonymous referee, and the staffs at Hull University Archive, the Public Record Office and the British Library.

2   *The Glasgow Mechanics Magazine*, no. xxxii, as quoted in Jennings, H. (ed.) (1985) *Pandemonium 1660–1886: The Coming of the Machine as Seen by Contemporary Observers.* London: Deutsch, p 164.

3   Lyon, D. (2002) Surveillance Studies: Understanding Visibility, Mobility and the Phenetic Fix, *Surveillance and Society*, Vol. 1, No. 1, p 4.

4   For a brief introduction to the wider theoretical ramifications of the 'surveillance society', see the section 'Visions of Surveillance' in Norris, C. and Armstrong, G. (1999) *The Maximum Surveillance Society: The Rise of CCTV.* Oxford: Berg, pp 3–10. A more dynamic approach to the definition of surveillance and its ostensibly 'new' developments can be found in Marx, G. (2002) What's New About the 'New Surveillance'? Classifying Change and Continuity, *Surveillance and Society*, Vol. 1, No. 1, pp 9–29.

5   See, for example, Moran, J. (1998) A Brief Chronology of Photographic and Video Surveillance, in Norris, C., Moran, J. and Armstrong, G. (eds), *Surveillance, Closed Circuit Television and Social Control.* Aldershot: Ashgate, pp 277–87, at p 280, which credits Bournemouth with the UK's first public CCTV system in 1985; Davies, S. (1996) *Big Brother.* London: Pan, p 186, dates it to 1985 and the explosion of CCTV in football grounds financed by the Football Trust.

6   Manwaring-White, S. (1983) *The Policing Revolution: Police Technology, Democracy and Liberty in Britain.* Brighton: Harvester, pp 70–1, at p 51.

7   Hesse, L. (2002) The Transition from Video Motion Detection to Intelligent Scene Discrimination and Target Tracking in Automated Video Surveillance Systems, *Security Journal*, Vol. 15, No. 2, pp 69–78, at p 78.

8   Norris and Armstrong, op. cit., pp 51–2.

9   Emsley, C. (1996) *The English Police: A Political and Social History.* London: Longman, pp 224–5. For a discussion on how this relates to the wider concept of surveillance, see *inter alia* Neocleous, M. (2000) *The Fabrication of Social Order: A Critical Theory of Police Power.* London: Pluto Press, pp 49–51.

10   *Regulations for the day patrol and watchmen of the Edinburgh police establishment* (1838). Edinburgh: Oliver & Boyd, p 5; 'The New Police Instructions', *The Times*, 25 September 1829.

11   Weiner, M.J. (1990) *Reconstructing the Criminal: Culture, Law and Policy in England 1830–1914*. Cambridge: Cambridge University Press, pp 101, 148, 149.

12   Public Record Office (PRO), Home Office (HO) 45/5734, 'Police surveillance of liberated prisoners in France' (1854).

13   PRO Prison Commission (PCOM) 7/276, 'Habitual Criminals Registry: removal from Home Office to Metropolitan Police Office' (1895–1896).

14   Ireland, R.W. (2002) The Felon and the Angel Copier: Criminal Identity and the Promise of Photography in Victorian England and Wales, in Knafla, L. (ed.), *Policing and War in Europe*. Westport, CT: Greenwood Press, pp 53–86, p 77. See also Sekula, A. (1986) 'The Body and the Archive', *October*, 39, pp 3–64.

15   Scott, H. (1954) *Scotland Yard*. London: André Deutsch, pp 130, 136.

16   Miller, W. (1984) 'Police Authority in London and New York City 1830–1870', in Emsley, C. (ed.), *Essays in Comparative History: Economy, Politics and Society in Britain and America 1850–1920*. Milton Keynes: Open University Press, pp 209–25, p 213.

17   Emsley, C. (1993) 'Mother, what *did* policeman do when there weren't any motors?' The Law, the Police and the Regulation of Motor Traffic in England 1900–1939, *Historical Journal*, Vol. 36, No. 2, pp 357–81; Weinberger, B. (1995) *The Best Police in the World: An Oral History of English Policing from the 1930s to the 1960s*. Aldershot: Scolar.

18   Constant, E. (1987) The Social Locus of Technological Practice: Community, System or Organisation?, in Bijker, W.E., Hughes, T.P. and Pinch, T.J. (eds), *The Social Construction of Technological Systems: New Directions in the Sociology and History of Technology*. Cambridge, MA: MIT Press, pp 223–42, at p 228. The social construction of technology (SCOT) approach is summed up by Graham, S. and Marvin, S. (1996) *Telecommunications and the City: Electronic Spaces, Urban Places*. London: Routledge, pp 104–7.

19   PRO Metropolitan Police (MEPO) 2/2507, 'Palestine police and wireless', Letter of Metropolitan Police secretary in answer to Palestine Police query, 16 December 1938; MEPO 2/5368, 'Staff required for Operation, Map, and Information Rooms', Commissioner to Home Office, 11 May 1934.

20   MEPO 2/5368, Commissioner to Home Office, 27 January 1936.

21   MEPO 2/5368, Minute from Chief Inspector, D.1 branch, 23 February 1935.

22   Ashmore, E. (1927) Anti-Aircraft Defence, *Royal United Service Institution Journal*, Vol. 72, p 10; Smith, M. (1984) *British Air Strategy Between the Wars*. Oxford: Clarendon Press, pp 73, 190; Terraine, J. (1982) *White Heat: The New Warfare 1914–18*. London: Sidgwick & Jackson, pp 270–1.

23   MEPO 2/5368, Memo to Supt, Communications Dept, 17 June 1936.

24   MEPO 2/5368, Minute from Commissioner Trenchard, 1 February 1935.

25   Marx, op. cit., p 23.

26   Ericson, R.V. and Haggerty, D. (1997) *Policing the Risk Society*. Oxford: Clarendon Press, pp 389–90.

27   MEPO 2/8007, Suggested use of television for police purposes, 6 November 1947.

28   MEPO 2/9956, 'Use of closed-circuit television by police for traffic control and crime detection 1960–1969', 'Closed-Circuit Television' report to Research and Planning Branch, 16 March 1965.

29   Rawlings, P. (2002) *Policing: A Short History*. Cullompton: Willan, pp 199–200; Critchley, T.A. (1967) *A History of Police in England and Wales: 1900–1966*. London: Constable, pp 255–6.

30   MEPO 2/9956, Notes of a meeting held to discuss use of closed-circuit television, contribution by Detective Superintendent Cudmore, 12 January 1961.

31   Police Equipment Exhibition, *Police Review*, LXVIII, 3514, 20 May 1960, p 394.

32   Zworykin, V. (1958) *Television in Science and Industry*. London: Chapman & Hall, pp 190–3, 249–51.

33   MEPO 2/9956, 'Police Equipment Exhibition 1960', extract from report submitted by Superintendent Preece, V Division.

34   MEPO 2/9956, Minute of 16 August 1960.

35   MEPO 2/9956, Minute from Assistant Commissioner Douglas Webb, 16 August 1960.

36   MEPO 2/9956, Notes of a meeting held to discuss use of closed-circuit television, contribution of Detective Superintendent Gale, 12 January 1961.

37   HO 377/15, 'Report on a visit to Liverpool City Police Force 18–20 January 1965'; HO 377/16, 'Supplementary Report on the Experimental Use of Television Camera and Commando Police Patrolling by Liverpool City Police' (February 1966); Third Eye on Patrol, *The Times*, 14 November 1964.

38   Balmer, H. (1965) Cameras and Commandos Halve Liverpool's Crime, *Security Gazette*, February.

39   HO 377/15, p 2.

40   Experimental Detection by TV in the Dark, *The Times*, 17 February 1965; HO 377/15; HO 377/16.

41   HO 377/15, p 6.

42   HO 287/1498, 'Use of closed circuit television by police: national survey 1969', p 24.

43   MEPO 2/9956, Closed circuit television experiment in Hatton Garden, Report of Detective Inspector Thompson.

44   MEPO 2/9956, Report to Deputy Commander, Research and Planning, 11 October 1965.

45   MEPO 2/9956, Minute of 10 February 1966.

46   MEPO 2/2507, Letter of Metropolitan Police secretary in answer to Palestine Police query, 16 December 1938.

47   TV in Watch for Rail Vandals, *The Times*, 25 June 1965.

48   MEPO 2/956, Letter from Home Office to Commissioner, 19 December 1966.

49   TV cameras help London fight against crime, *The Times*, 4 January 1968.

50   MEPO 2/9956, Memo from Commander 'A' (Operations), 1 August 1968.

51   Ericson and Haggerty, op. cit., p 35.

52   MEPO 2/9956, Report from A8 Branch, 30 October 1968.

53   National Council for Civil Liberties Archive, University of Hull, DCL 459/8, Letter from T. Smythe to J. Callaghan, 27 October 1968.

54   Waddington, P.A.J. (1993) Dying in a Ditch: The Use of Police Powers in Public Order, *International Journal of the Sociology of Law*, Vol. 21, pp 335–53, at p 342.

55   HO 287/1498, 33b, p 7.

56   Big Brother Is Watching You, *The Times*, 31 June 1973, p 14. This claim has been interpreted by Fay as an example of the 'mutability' of CCTV systems. In fact, as the record demonstrates, these cameras were primarily intended for crowd control. Fay, S. (1998) Tough on Crime, Tough on Civil Liberties: Some Negative Aspects of Britain's Wholesale Adoption of CCTV Surveillance during the 1990s, *International Review of Law, Computers and Technology*, Vol. 12, No. 2, pp 315–46, at p 325.

57   HO 287/1498.

58   Constant, op. cit., p 230.

59   Graham and Marvin, op. cit., pp 94–101.

60   Coleman, R. and Sim, J. (2000) 'You'll never walk alone': CCTV Surveillance, Order and Neo-liberal Rule in Liverpool City Centre, *British Journal of Sociology*, Vol. 51, No. 4, pp 623–39.

61   McCahill, M. (2002) *The Surveillance Web: The Rise of Visual Surveillance in an English City*. Cullompton: Willan, pp 181–2.

62   Thrift, N. (1996) New Urban Eras and Old Technological Fears: Reconfiguring the Goodwill of Electronic Things, *Urban Studies*, Vol. 22, No. 8, pp 1463–93, at pp 1468–9.

63   Marx, op. cit., pp 9, 28–9.

64   Latour, B. (1987) *Science in Action: How to Follow Scientists and Engineers Through Society*. Milton Keynes: Open University Press, pp 227, 232, 259.

Chapter 3

Multiple Targets: The Reasons to Support Town-centre CCTV Systems

David Mackay[1]

Little attempt has been made to investigate the reasons for supporting town-centre CCTV systems. Attention has normally focused on crime reduction and potential infringement of civil liberties. This essay concentrates on the public reasons that have been given for supporting it.

The reasons behind this support are studied and examples are produced; these have seldom attracted headlines but form the basis for the support given by all partners. The study shows that CCTV was sold as a political response to the law and order debate. Its true purpose is shown to be an amalgam of dealing with public disorder, the fear of crime, improving economic benefits and town centre management issues. All of these relate to self-interest on the part of the supporters. These findings are confirmed after a series of non-structured interviews in the case study.

Introduction

Most people in the CCTV sector are familiar with the plethora of conflicting claims regarding the effectiveness of town-centre CCTV systems. These claims seem to revolve around a single theme, namely that CCTV either 'works' to reduce crime in the locality or that it does not 'work'. The 'owners', i.e. the local authority and the police, usually state that town-centre CCTV systems certainly make the area safer, reduce crime and reduce the fear of crime. This opinion is constantly reinforced, especially by the media, who ignore any inconvenient facts to the contrary, even when they are produced by the Home Office.[2]

The situation appears to be one of hotly disputed claims and counterclaims, with little evidence that town-centre CCTV systems have lived up to their original claims regarding their potential beneficial effects on crime, fear of crime and increased public confidence. For their part, the general public clearly want the systems to work and they want something to be done about crime and the fear of crime. Therefore, apart from the reservations expressed by academics, town-centre CCTV systems have all the appearances of a self-fulfilling prophecy. These optimistic claims have been accepted without demur by the media and public, thus providing the standard premise that 'CCTV achieves the results claimed for it'.[3]

This begs the question that there must be better reasons for supporting CCTV than this impasse. Surely there must be some points of agreement to justify the continuing expenditure? A closer look, however, shows that the supporters of town-centre CCTV systems have regularly made a number of other claims relating to public opinion in favour of CCTV, the economic well-being of the local area and its use in improving the image of the local area.[4] Yet, these matters have never received the same coverage as crime statistics or funding.

The general view of town-centre CCTV systems is the 'police paramount' approach. This regards CCTV as a means of preventing, investigating and generally keeping an eye on offending behaviour and it has tended to dominate all evaluation of town-centre CCTV systems. Such an outlook has consistently diminished the relevance of the other reasons claimed for installing CCTV in the first instance.

No process exists for measuring its impact on these matters and therefore vague, positive comments were normally substituted instead of facts and figures. When local project evaluations failed to support these claims, changes were made to the 'results' claimed—a classic 'spin' operation. Town-centre CCTV systems do not openly admit that they have failed to perform against their original expectations; instead this is ignored and other beneficial effects are subsequently claimed.[5]

Research outline

The research project studied the decision-making process involved in the development of local authority-sponsored town-centre CCTV systems. This included those systems where the local authority is the principal supporter in a local partnership that includes the police, the private sector and crime reduction or community safety groups. It investigated the relative influences of various factors, including the availability of central government funding, and reviewed the wide variety of benefits claimed for town-centre CCTV systems. Crime reduction statistics were not examined in detail.

There are four main partners or stakeholders in town-centre CCTV systems: the local authority, the police, local businesses and the local media. The actions and attitudes of these groups have been investigated across many town-centre CCTV projects in the UK over recent years. The case study examined the role of the stakeholders in the Glasgow CityWatch system and noted their reasons for supporting the project. The case study was a qualitative survey, and in-depth interviews were conducted with relevant senior staff who had been involved in the project; they were as follows:

- CCTV manager: in control of all council CCTV strategy;

- senior council officer: chairman of the CityWatch Association for six years;

- retail manager: chairman of the City Centre Association;

- press officer: press officer for the CityWatch Association;

- senior police officer: the force CCTV liaison officer;

- town centre manager: operations manager for the City Centre Partnership (CCP);

- SLGIU: research officer for the Scottish Local Government Information Unit (SLGIU).

The constant question posed throughout the research project was: 'why are town-centre CCTV systems so popular?' The standard response is that they are good crime-prevention measures. In fact, there is very little undisputed evidence to support this claim. Any available evidence tends to suggest that it has had a minimal crime prevention effect and only works when part of a package of crime prevention measures.[6] This has been a common theme of all CCTV research and a wide range of other studies have shown similar results.[7] Regardless of this caveat, town-centre CCTV systems are strongly supported by local partnerships and central government.

History

Town-centre CCTV systems are a situational crime prevention measure and have been deployed to tackle concerns over crime, image and economic benefits in a local area. The latter two are directly linked to social disorder, i.e. violent and property crime, vagrancy, graffiti, public drunkenness and begging. The long-term impact of social disorder has been identified as one of the prime reasons driving middle-class people out of inner cities and thereby reducing the economic benefit to the area.[8] Disorder is suggested by vandalism, which feeds the fear of crime. This in turn is interpreted as an indicator of rising crime, thus bringing economic disbenefit in its wake.[9] In recent years, these matters have also been tackled by 'zero tolerance' campaigns.

It is interesting to note that central government had enumerated this multi-benefits vision of town-centre CCTV's role as early as 1993. They listed the primary objectives of CCTV schemes as: 'To achieve a reduction in the rate of crime; to reduce the public's fear of crime; increase business takings; protect public areas and bring them back into general use; and help ease police manpower difficulties.'[10] Early schemes, such as Nottingham and Birmingham, stated this and the Glasgow CityWatch objectives were also similar:

- To cut crime and vandalism by 25 per cent.

- To reduce the fear of crime.

- To bring in £40 million additional income from increased visitors.

- To create 1,500 extra jobs within the City Centre.

- To attract 225,000 extra people per year to the City Centre.

The Glasgow project was managed by the CityWatch Association, a public-private partnership involving the Glasgow Development Agency (GDA), Strathclyde Regional Council, Glasgow City Council, Glasgow Chamber of Commerce, Marks & Spencer, Britannia Life and Strathclyde Police. This collaboration was part of a national trend that has led to the rise of the mixed sector in British politics[11] and was a direct response to the central government aim of building partnerships to combat crime.[12] The project received overwhelming public backing and this gave GCC a very good reason to support CCTV.[13] Over the lifetime of the project, all of Glasgow CityWatch's aims can claim to have been achieved, although, as always, there is disagreement over its crime reduction impact.

Despite a rise in recorded crime in the police division partly covered by CityWatch,[14] Strathclyde Police still regard CCTV as a 'valuable weapon in the fight against crime', and believe that it has an important role by the 'enhanced sense of community safety it brings'. However, surveys show that CCTV did not make people feel safer in Glasgow city centre,[15] in marked contrast with the chief constable's claim that 'CCTV is pivotal in generating the 'feel-good factor' and assisting in reducing the fear of crime'.

Financial reasons

The UK makes the most use of town-centre CCTV systems of any member state of the EU and the government has provided more than £205 million to support 1,400 town-centre CCTV projects since 1994.[16] Local partnerships have spent a similar amount of matching funding and are currently struggling to meet annual running costs estimated at £50 million. So positive has central government support been that, by 1997, the bulk of Home Office expenditure on crime prevention was being spent on CCTV in public places.[17]

The research confirms that central government funding is used to coax local authorities to carry out a political programme. The SLGIU describe the availability of central government funding as a 'perverse incentive' for local authorities, that can be used as a lever for bringing in additional outside funding. They consider this to be a common theme in local government and it is done mainly because of the political plaudits it earns locally. Other partners, such as the police, will support projects once it is known that others will also share the project costs, as indicated by Strathclyde Police in 1993.[18]

The spread of funding sources across the public and private sectors is also welcomed by central government, which did not wish to pay huge costs for this technological solution.[19] This is the common theme surrounding all discussions of CCTV project funding, namely that others must also share the costs. The implementation of a Crime Reduction Programme, including CCTV, now enhances the opportunity for local crime and disorder partnerships to win central government funding to tackle crime.[20] Regardless of these statutory funds, the provision of funding is believed to be the responsibility of the local authority and this is the strongly held opinion of the business sector, as expressed by the retail manager.

There has always been a strong suspicion that the effectiveness of CCTV systems has been 'talked up' to justify the expenditure involved and support bids for further central government funding. When local project evaluation did not support the original objectives, significant changes were made to 'results' claimed by the systems. However, none of these 'results' have been subjected to independent scrutiny and there is 'little scientific evidence to support these claims'.[21] None of these adverse research findings appear to have made much impact on the overall support for CCTV.

The primary funding sources for town-centre CCTV schemes are as follows: the local authority, the police budget, the business community, the Home Office, the Scottish Office/Executive, the Welsh Office, the Northern Ireland Executive and, occasionally, Local Development Agencies. The secondary funding source is European Funds, successfully accessed, for example, by Swale Borough Council where CCTV formed part of a wider regeneration project.

Economic benefits

From their inception in the late 1980s, public-area CCTV systems were claimed to be the cure for various crime and social problems, as well as addressing issues affecting the local economy. The link between crime and economic disadvantage has been investigated by many towns, e.g. King's Lynn, Liverpool and Newcastle, and all came to the conclusion that town-centre CCTV could be employed to gain an economic advantage.[22] This economic benefit was conveniently linked to the business community's acceptance of the enlightened self-interest argument, namely that they should satisfy public expectations regarding social responsibility.

Crime is a real worry for local businesses as crime and fear of crime have adverse implications for local economies. If city centres are not fully used, they become run-down and threatening places, whereas out-of-town centres and shopping malls offer a greater feeling of safety.[23] Public-space CCTV attracts strong support, as it appears to offer solutions to local economic decline by deterring crime and increasing economic benefits. It is regarded as an investment towards the future development and well-being of an area. Influential bodies, such as the Local Government Association, believe that the revitalization of city centres is a major reason to support CCTV systems as this will result in economic advantage and the creation of a 'feel-good' factor.[24] Town-centre CCTV was introduced to Liverpool as part of a coordinated effort to bring people back into the city centre by making them feel safer. Even towns with low or declining crime rates, like Glasgow and Fleet, have introduced town-centre CCTV systems to counter the fear of crime and attract shoppers to the area.[25]

Local authorities, businesses and the media believe that there are economic benefits to be gained by supporting CCTV systems. Coventry Council stated that they supported it because of its ability to tackle the issues of crime and economic downturn cheaply. This is an example of the solid proof that commercial pressures play a major part in town-centre CCTV decisions.[26] Southampton's objective was to promote the city centre as an 'accessible, safe and high quality environment'. This desire to gain economic benefit from public-area CCTV is a common idea, even in the USA, where previous experience to the contrary was disregarded in New Jersey.[27] In Glasgow, the City Centre Partnership has also promoted the positive effects of CCTV and believes that it has created a 'a safer trading environment for businesses'.

Cities are in competition with one another and need their own unique selling point (USP),[28] and the business sector supports town-centre CCTV systems solely on the basis of commercial benefit, a point confirmed by the case study retail manager. He emphasized the business community's belief that town-centre CCTV systems perform the same role as advertising and brand building, by sending a positive signal that the location is working hard to maintain its competitive position. These matters of image are regarded as critical by the commercial sector,[29] which considers that the main operational priorities of CCTV are to prevent vandalism and graffiti, to manage traffic and parking, and to maintain a pleasant environment.

In Glasgow's case, these claims for economic benefit can be shown to be successful, as city centre employment has increased by 30,000 jobs since the introduction of its main CCTV system. According to the senior council officer, this appears to endorse their original support for the project, which aimed to increase employment in the area. Nevertheless, it is difficult to convince town centre businesses to contribute to the costs, as they regard profitability as far more important than crime prevention; regardless of this, local authorities are very supportive of the demands from local business for public-space CCTV systems.[30]

Public opinion

Public opinion plays a major role in determining support for town-centre CCTV systems. The Home Office reported strong public support, in 1992, for the installation of public-space CCTV cameras and because of this, extravagant claims were made for CCTV.[31] A survey conducted in 1993 reported 90 per cent public support for open-street CCTV in Glasgow city centre. Although subsequent research reduced this figure to 67 per cent, the 90 per cent figure still retains its iconic status in this respect.[32] Glasgow City Council knew about the strong public support for the system and was therefore fully aware of the political problems that would be caused by pulling the plug on it. This situation was described as a form of entrapment by the senior council officer—'public opinion supports it and we must agree with this.'

The local media has a prominent role in shaping public opinion and has fully supported town-centre CCTV systems. There is a symbiotic relationship between the media and politicians, as the media need 'copy' and the politicians need the media to transmit their views.[33] The press officer noted that this positive political message has enabled the media to propagate 'good news' stories about town-centre CCTV systems, and in this way, both media and politicians service their own interests.

The media is seen as a strong advocate of the overriding utility of town-centre CCTV systems.[34] The local press reports on local crime, and regularly suggests CCTV as a possible solution, thus starting the ball rolling.[35] This support continues over time and it constantly reinforces the benefits of town-centre CCTV systems ('thug caught on camera', etc.). The press officer regards this as part of a complicity in promoting CCTV as a 'good thing', simply because it is regarded as a 'good thing' with an excellent local 'feel-good' message. This scepticism has also been noted by other researchers, who believe that as the general public only have 'partial', i.e. positively biased, information available about CCTV, it is not therefore surprising that they support the concept.[36]

The local community and the local police agree that CCTV is a 'good thing' and fully support it. As there are expectations that the city centre needs to be fully equipped to meet modern-day expectations, the retail manager claims that the absence of a CCTV system will result in the public asking 'why not?' The senior council officer pointed out that the council needed to 'do something' to reduce the fear of crime. This need to be seen to 'do something' about crime in response to public opinion is consistently identified as a common motivation and town-centre CCTV is also believed to create a 'feel good' factor about the area.[37]

The significance of public opinion was emphasized by the SLGIU. 'Feel good' matters take precedence over all measurable effects of town-centre CCTV systems, as it is important to politicians to keep the electorate happy. As a result, ' "happiness for all" is the sub-text followed by central and local government.' In reality, this 'feel-good' factor is a fictitious concept. There is no evidence to support such claims, and this is also the case with the fear of crime, which is another chimera that cannot be objectively measured. Town-centre CCTV systems are attractive to the partners as they are a response to public opinion and give an impression that 'something is being done' to combat the fear of crime, the belief in which has almost become pathological.[38]

Partnership building

The rise of local partnerships has been a feature of central government's aim of building partnerships to combat crime,[39] and a partnership with other interested groups, e.g. police and traders is the most common method of local authority involvement in town-centre CCTV systems. Partnerships are the best method of attracting funding as each member may have access to specific funding unavailable to other members. That this is normal cultural behaviour for local authorities, is confirmed by the SLGIU Research Officer. In addition businesses now believe it is advantageous to act in the best interests of society by linking business and the community and thus they support various 'soft' causes; town-centre CCTV comes into this category.[40]

The business ethos of supporting the community is a strong force and town-centre CCTV is a good 'soft' cause for them. Local businesses have been a major force in the expansion of town-centre CCTV systems and in recent years they have been heavily involved in forming partnerships, including local councils and the private sector, to promote the good management of town centres.[41] This approach has been fully backed by the Association of Town Centre Management, which recognizes that partnerships are an 'essential pre-condition of successful town centre initiatives'.

Town-centre CCTV systems are popular with the various partners, therefore councils such as Glasgow and Southend were able to use this partnership structure to address some of their community safety issues.[42] The police used the introduction of urban regeneration initiatives to promote the idea of using other agencies in the fight against crime, instead of just regarding it as a police matter. The senior police officer pointed out that, as town-centre CCTV systems could only be established with the support of other organizations, its partnership structure enabled the police to focus other organizations on the police's chosen priorities. When Glasgow City Council eventually implemented a strategic review of its town-centre CCTV systems in 2001, its report recommended a partnership solution, with eight control rooms migrating to a single, super monitoring station by May 2003.

Management capabilities

Town-centre CCTV systems have been recognized as a practical management aid by all of the partners. Both Gras[43] and Davies[44] have noted the value of town-centre CCTV systems as an operational management tool for the police and this was endorsed by the Chief Constable of Strathclyde Police, who described it as 'an excellent community safety tool'.[45] These operational management benefits make life considerably easier in police control rooms. CCTV can make a useful contribution towards achieving key performance indicators, such as response to '999' calls, which are directly linked to central funding for police authorities. Whereas the police are enthusiastic for the establishment of town-centre CCTV systems, resource-based police support is dependent on the attitude and priorities of the local chief constable. In reality, by giving assistance in kind, the police have, in most cases, been able to assume full operational control of the project with minimal financial contribution.

Although crime prevention was not mentioned in any significant fashion, the police believe CCTV is particularly useful in providing evidence when possible witnesses would be too scared to testify. Financial savings are also a reason for police support for town-centre CCTV systems as court costs can be dramatically reduced by a 'guilty' plea.[46] The use of recorded CCTV evidence is claimed to have encouraged many guilty pleas, and cost saving is a constant theme of police support for town-centre CCTV systems. Obviously, financial savings are a prime reason for the police to support CCTV systems.

Town-centre CCTV systems are able to assist with the problems over the deployment of police resources. According to the senior police officer, CCTV observation provides verification of the actual situation on the ground and this allows the police control room to decide on the level of police response required; traffic congestion is another matter that can also be tackled. CCTV is versatile and new aspects are constantly being discovered—for instance, public order situations can be better and more efficiently controlled.

But, above all, town-centre CCTV provides archive recordings. The senior police officer pointed out that the police are faced with a lack of information about incidents and also lose evidence because of witness fears. CCTV recording prevents this and is normally best evidence; it is a third-party source and is the only evidence in court that does not have an obvious agenda.

Town-centre management is also enhanced by the flexibility of CCTV systems. The town centre manager drew attention to numerous instances of camera information being used positively assisting shoppers, finding lost persons, summoning ambulances, etc. This practical assistance was corroborated by the senior council officer's observation that council officials can view town centre cameras and identify litter, flyposting, etc. In other examples, Portsmouth council has said that its town-centre CCTV system is 'just one tool with many spin-offs, not just for dealing with crime, but other city management issues too',[47] and Sutton council has stated that 'CCTV isn't just about crime statistics'.

Conclusion

The overwhelming impression from the case study is that decisions are taken to support town-centre CCTV systems solely on the basis that it will assist in a variety of matters that are considered to be important by the decision-makers. All of these play a major part in the day-to-day concerns of the partners. These are very important aspects of improving the local area and its economic benefit. Significantly, there is little claim by any of the partners, including the police, that town-centre CCTV systems must be supported because they help to reduce crime. The research found that the various stakeholders (i.e. local authority, police, media and businesses) all protected their own interests by supporting the interlinked aims of crime prevention and economic benefit.

There is no evidence of any long-term philosophy that CCTV systems are important crime prevention measures; instead, expediency and self-interest are paramount. However, all of these self-interest activities are important to the local community and fully merit support. The research constantly reinforces the fact that self-interest takes precedence over any wider considerations.

Town-centre CCTV systems are supported because they will assist in tackling a range of important local concerns based on a series of considerations, namely financial implications, economic benefit, public opinion, partnership building and management of town centres. The case study focused on the Glasgow CityWatch system, where the reasons were found to be similar to those put forward over the past decade by the supporters of town-centre CCTV systems elsewhere in the UK. Central government funding is being used to entice local authorities to carry out a central government political programme. It gives an impression that 'something is being done' and local government has thereby gained additional funding. In the final analysis, the local authority, the police, the private sector and the media all gain from the catalyst of town-centre CCTV systems; according to the press officer, it is an all-round 'win–win' situation.

Notes

1   The author was Project Manager of the Glasgow CityWatch system from August 1994 until August 1996. The research project was presented as his dissertation for the MSc in Security Management at the Scarman Centre, University of Leicester. E-mail: dm@david-mackay.co.uk.

2   Norris, C. and Armstrong, A. (1999) *The Maximum Surveillance Society: The Rise of CCTV*. Oxford: Berg, p 65.

3   Ibid., p 9.

4   Drury, I. (2001) Tackling Car Crime: Southampton's Sharp End Surveillance Approach, *CCTV Today*, May, pp 47–9.

5   Ditton, J., Short, E., Phillips, S., Norris, C. and Armstrong, G. (1999) *The Effect of Closed Circuit Television on Recorded Crime Rates and Public Concern about Crime in Glasgow*. Edinburgh: Stationery Office, pp 57–8.

6   Tilley, N. (1993) *Understanding Car Parks, Crime and CCTV: Evaluation Lessons from Safer Cities*, Crime Prevention Unit Series Paper 42. London: Home Office, pp 23–5.

7   Webb, A. and Laycock, G. (1992) *Reducing Crime on the London Underground: An Evaluation of Three Pilot Projects*, Crime Prevention Unit Paper No. 30. London: Home Office, p 6.

8   Fukuyama, F. (1999) *The Great Disruption: Human Nature and the Reconstitution of Social Order*. London: Profile, p 125.

9   Barker, M. and Bridgeman, C. (1994) *Preventing Vandalism: What Works?*, Police Research Group, Crime Detection and Prevention Series, Paper No. 56. London. Home Office, p 4.

10   The Scottish Office Home and Health Department Research Specification 'Closed Circuit Television in City Centres in Scotland', letter to CityWatch, from Scottish Office Central Research Unit, 25 November 1994.

11   Stoker, G. (1991) *The Politics of Local Government*, 2nd edn. London: Macmillan, pp 93 and 226.

12   Internal Memorandum, EMC00317.033, 18 March 1993, Scottish Office.

13   Ditton, J. (2000) Crime and the City: Public Attitudes towards Open-Street CCTV in Glasgow, *British Journal of Criminology*, Vol. 40, pp 693 and 705.

14   Strathclyde Police Annual Reports: 1997–98; 1998–99; 1999–2000; 2000–01.

15   Ditton, op. cit., pp 692–709.

16   (a) 'CCTV Funding Applications Key Statistics', letter to author from Crime Reduction Programme Unit, Home Office, 24 October 2001; (b) letter to author from Scottish Executive Justice Department Crime Prevention Unit, 21 November 2001; (c) More Cameras, New Recording Rules in Ulster, *Professional Security*, website, *http://www.professionalsecurity.co.uk/Files/Archive/ archiveframe.html*, 31 October 2001.

17   Pease, K. (1997) Crime Prevention, in Maguire, M., Morgan, R. and Reiner, R. (eds), *The Oxford Handbook of Criminology*, 2nd edn. Oxford: Oxford University Press, p 971.

18   Letter from Chief Constable Strathclyde Police to Assistant Chief Executive, Strathclyde Regional Council, 12 July 1993.

19   Dearlove, J. and Saunders, P. (2000) *Introduction to British Politics*, 3rd edn. Cambridge: Polity, p 649.

20   Curtin, L., Tilley, N., Owens, M. and Pease, K. (2001) *Developing Crime Reduction Plans: Some Examples from the Reducing Burglary Initiative*, Briefing Note on Crime Reduction Research Paper No. 7. London: Home Office, p 1.

21   Phillips, C. (1999) A Review of CCTV Evaluations: Crime Reduction Effects and Attitudes towards Its Use, in Painter, K. and Tilley, N. (eds), *Seeing and Being Seen to Prevent Crime*, Crime Prevention Studies, Vol. 10. Monsey, NY: Criminal Justice Press, pp 123–55.

22   Gras, M. (2001) *Beyond Crime and Fear of Crime Reduction: Side Effects as Main Effects of CCTV?* Paper to Euro Conference Lecture, 29 April 2001.

23   Drake, G. and Lee, C. (2000) *The Urban Challenge*. London: Hodder & Stoughton Educational, pp 64–76.

24   Charlesworth, Z. (1997) 'Foreword', *CCTV Directory 1997/98*. London: Local Government Association, quoted in Gras, op. cit.

25   Arlidge, J. (1994) 'True Stories, Welcome Big Brother', *The Independent*, 2 November, quoted in Gras, op. cit.

26   Norris and Armstrong, op. cit., p 8.

27      $2 million CCTV system for Jersey City, USA, *CCTVision*, July 2001, p 35.

28   Drake and Lee, op. cit., p 76.

29   Ibid., p 68.

30   Phillips, op. cit.

31   Carr (1992), quoted in Gill, M. (ed.) (1994) *Crime at Work: Studies in Security and Crime Prevention*, Vol. I. Leicester: Perpetuity Press, p 187.

32   Ditton, op. cit., pp 693 and 705.

33   Kavanagh, D. (1996) *British Politics: Continuity and Change*, 3rd edn. Oxford: Oxford University Press, p 207.

34   Norris and Armstrong, op. cit., pp 70–88.

35   Davies, S. (1996) *Big Brother: Britain's Web of Surveillance and the New Technological Order*. London: Pan, p 189.

36   Honess, T. and Charman, E. (1992) *Closed Circuit Television in Public Places*, Crime Prevention Unit Series Paper 35. London: Home Office, p 25.

37   Gill, M. (1996) Interview, in *Security Industry*, October 1996, pp 81–2.

38   Davies, op. cit., p 201.

39   Scottish Office (1993) Internal Memorandum, EMC00317.033, 18 March 1993, Scottish Office.

40   Bartol, K. and Martin, D. (1998) *Management*. Boston: McGraw-Hill, p 104.

41   Norris and Armstrong, op. cit., p 39.

42   'CCTV in Southend', *CCTVision*, July 2001, pp 18–20.

43   Gras, op. cit.

44   Davies, op. cit., p 174.

45   Strathclyde Police (2001) Report of the Chief Constable of Strathclyde Police 2000/2001, p 35.

46   Harries, R. (1999) *The Cost of Criminal Justice*, Home Office Development and Statistics Directorate, Research Findings No. 103, pp 1–3.

47   Portsmouth Deploys Initial 30+ Cameras as 'City Management Tool', *CCTV Today*, Vol. 3, No. 2, 1996, p 6.

Chapter 4

Lessons in Implementing CCTV Schemes: An Early Review

Polly Smith, Angela Spriggs, Javier Argomaniz, Jenna Allen, Patricia Jessiman, Deena Kara, Ross Little, Daniel Swain, Matt Follett and Martin Gill[1]

This chapter seeks to identify early lessons in good practice in the design and implementation phases of CCTV schemes. It is intended for use by policy-makers, academics and practitioners alike. The research indicates weaknesses in the initial bidding phase, primarily in the quality of data and analysis available to partnerships as well as the theoretical basis behind the use of CCTV as a crime prevention mechanism. The paper underlines the importance of community consultation and the development of accountability mechanisms, and discusses the practical problems that occur in the implementation process. The conclusion offers tentative proposals for change.

Introduction

While all CCTV schemes that received government funding under the Crime Reduction Initiative (CRI) are to be evaluated, the Home Office sought an independent evaluation of 17 projects comprising 93 individual schemes located in town and city centres, car parks, hospitals, recreation spaces and residential areas. This chapter is based on an early stage review of issues relating to the ways schemes had been implemented, recognizing that some were still at the planning stage. One project did not meet the evaluation timetable and was subsequently dropped.

The paper discusses a range of issues beginning with an outline of the partnerships and agencies involved. Here, the way in which partnerships cooperate in the implementation of CCTV is discussed. Next, the paper reviews the methods adopted by these partnerships to justify the case for CCTV during the bidding stage. The quality of consultation with the recipients of CCTV at all stages of the implementation process is addressed. The paper also outlines the problems that partnerships face when dealing with the design and installation of CCTV, bearing in mind the complex technology involved. Finally, the paper discusses the way in which partnerships intend to meet the revenue costs of the schemes in the long term.

Partners and other agencies

Round 1 of the Crime Reduction Programme CCTV Initiative awarded £64 million across 352 schemes by November 2000, and soon after the Home Office announced a second round of bidding. Over 800 bids were submitted, and 332 schemes worth around £106 million were successful. The bids for funding were submitted in the name of Crime and Disorder Reduction Partnerships, which represent a multitude of agencies (police, local authority, housing, probation, health, education, etc.). However, it was usual for one or two agencies within the partnership to act as 'lead agencies' for the project as a whole. Commonly, a sub-group was created, involving only those agencies with a vested interest in the success of the scheme (with the local authority, police and housing most often represented). In practice, implementation was often managed by the staff of a single department within the local authority. Lead agent/s were left to 'get on with it' and report back to the sub-group, and subsequently the main partnership. Thus 'project management' and 'project managers' refers to those groups and individuals tasked with the implementation process, and not the Crime and Disorder Reduction Partnership.

Managing a project within a context of partnership working can present particular difficulties in addition to the usual challenges of project management. Within the schemes considered here, the most frequently encountered problems arose, firstly, from the fact that common priorities were not agreed and, secondly, from a lack of accountability mechanisms.

Different agencies may have the same general aims in terms of crime prevention but their specific priorities can be very different. For example, in one of the schemes the three main partners shared the overall aim of 'reducing crime and the fear of crime', but differed in their internal priorities. The local authority saw CCTV as a tool for improving the quality of life for residents, the housing association saw CCTV as an opportunity to enforce tenancy agreements, and the police wanted to use the scheme to enhance their ability to investigate reported crime. Differing objectives should be declared and differences resolved as early in the implementation process as possible if the optimal CCTV system is to be designed and implemented as a means of achieving those objectives.

It is particularly important for the lead agency to consult and make concrete agreements with other agencies upon which the success of the scheme will rely. For example, the lead agency may assume that the police will give a certain level of priority to calls coming out of the CCTV control room and will inform their operators and officers about the scheme. This does not always happen, which will considerably influence the effectiveness of the scheme. Assumptions such as these should be converted into concrete agreements (if possible) during the early stages of implementation.

The transfer of 'lead agency' status was not uncommon, either because different agencies had expertise in different parts of the development process or because priorities changed and strategic decisions were more appropriately taken elsewhere. Unless the different agencies shared the same priorities for a scheme, this could result in a radical change of design once lead agency status changed. Design changes proved costly both in terms of time and money, and may be better avoided if priorities are agreed at the start of the process.

For a project to be implemented effectively, relevant agencies and personnel need to be made accountable. A number of cases have been identified where progress was delayed because a key person or agency had not completed activities that it had undertaken, but the other partner members were not inclined or able to apply any pressure to get the task completed. Even in the case where a technical consultant or a builder has been employed under contract, partner agencies that are not party to the contract cannot enforce it and are therefore dependant upon good accountability mechanisms (even if these are usually informal) within the partnership as a whole. There should be opportunities to ascertain whether commitments have been fulfilled and mechanisms are in place to enforce performance or receive redress in the event of a failure.

Appraisal of the problem

Partnerships making an application for funding were required to identify the nature of the crime and disorder problem(s) which existed in the proposed intervention areas. The Home Office provided guidance for statutory partnerships outlining the criteria for selecting intervention areas (Home Office, 1999, section 4.3). This states that partnerships must paint 'a clear and detailed picture of the crime and disorder problem to be tackled set in its local social and physical context'. Furthermore, 'the cause of the problem and/or risk factors for offending [must] have been established, as a basis for designing the intervention'. Evidence was required to support the conclusions drawn about the nature of the problem. The evaluation has found serious weaknesses here that apply to most bids, not least in the identification of 'problem' areas and in the quality of data available to support the assertions made.

It might be expected that partnerships would have an area with crime and/or disorder problems in mind when proposing to put a crime prevention 'solution' in place. However, this is not necessarily what happens. From the projects under study, five processes emerged by which partnerships chose the areas for which they submitted bids. These are as follows:

1. A pre-existing crime or disorder problem which would benefit from the application of CCTV had been identified by a partnership before the funding became available.

2. Inspired by the availability of funding, a partnership sought to identify a crime problem that would benefit from the application of CCTV.

3. An area had been identified prior to the availability of funding, in which the partnership felt a need to demonstrate some sort of crime prevention activity to the local community. Inspired by the availability of CCTV funding, the partnership sought to show that the crime problems in this area would meet bid requirements.

4. The partnership believed that the presence of CCTV in an area would increase the likelihood that funding would be granted under future programmes. The partnership sought to identify an area that would meet bid requirements.

5. The partnership wished to bring money, of any kind, into its area and was prepared to risk the wasted effort of a failed bid in an attempt to achieve this. The partnership sought to identify an area that would meet bid requirements.

Therefore it can be seen that while there is in each case a requirement to show that proposed schemes would meet needs, this is not quite the linear or ordered process one might suppose. That is not to say that a crime problem did not exist in the areas chosen for CCTV funding, and one which CCTV could be expected to alleviate, but the order of events outlined in point 1 above was not always apparent.

> The experience of one project team in making a bid exemplifies this issue. The project manager said he viewed the CRI funding as an opportunity to placate the community that 'shouts loudest'. In this case, evidence was gathered to demonstrate that the preferred area met the criteria, rather than making an overall determination of which area was the most suitable.

An estate with greater problems was not made the subject of a bid because, he said, the local management team there were less active in its pursuit of funding.

As indicated in point 4 above, some partnerships believed that the presence of CCTV would increase the likelihood of success in future funding rounds. In two of the projects under study, this was explicitly given as a reason for bidding and is not a new finding. As Williams and Johnstone have noted, 'Other more lucrative central government funding such as that for urban generation, requires the provision of a safe environment and CCTV is usually turned to, to fulfil this role' (2000, p. 189). While it is necessary to be realistic about the world in which the various agencies operate, it is also necessary to point out these weak points in the bidding process.

Other than the motivation behind the identification of 'problem areas', the second significant weakness identified at the bidding stage was the quality of the data available to partnerships. In only a few cases was a staff member with knowledge of statistics and data analysis included in the project bidding team. It was more usual for a hard-pressed police or council data analyst to be required to come up with relevant statistics, and even then they were not always consulted about the most appropriate figures to use. Thus what was presented was more often those figures project managers thought best to present rather than using the expertise of the analysts to produce a more sophisticated analysis.

Providing data on areas which are not coterminous with existing boundaries (e.g. ward or police beat boundaries) has proved problematic for partnerships bidding for any type of funding, not just crime reduction initiatives. The commonly-used Crime and Disorder Audits and Index of Multiple Deprivation statistics are presented by electoral ward boundaries, and do not necessarily accurately describe deprivation levels in a smaller part of that ward where the CCTV scheme is to be functional. This is important because many wards contain a variety of types of housing, with the affluent and deprived living side by side. Some bids relied on police data, despite their well-known weaknesses. Others used public attitude surveys (especially fear of crime surveys), usually undertaken by local agencies, and many employed questionable methodologies that were inadequate for the task. The nature of these surveys is discussed at greater length below.

The passage of time can also cause problems. The time taken to formulate a solid bid, the consideration of bids, the acceptance of the bid and the receipt of funds mean that partnerships are liable to suffer from changes or fluctuations in both area context and crime trends. Once a bid is accepted, however, partnerships are unlikely to refuse the money simply because the crime problem has changed in nature or decreased in severity, and in most cases they would not know.

However, the Home Office discontinued the bidding process for CCTV funding in April 2003, introducing instead a single funding stream for crime reduction funding (including CAD (Communities Against Drugs), SCI (Safer Communities Initiative), PDF (Partnership Development Fund) and some DAT (Drugs

Action Team)). Crime Reduction Partnerships will be allocated money according to a formula, and it will be for the local partnerships to decide whether some of that money would be best spent on CCTV rather than some other crime reduction initiative.

Is CCTV the right solution?

The Home Office guidance for partnerships (Home Office, 1999, section 4.3) sets out the appropriate criteria for identifying a relevant crime prevention mechanism. The guidance states that 'the intervention [must follow] from theoretically sound crime reduction principles which suggest plausible causal mechanisms by which it could work against the current crime or disorder problem in the current context'. It is clear that many schemes did not understand the 'realist' terminology here (see Pawson and Tilley, 1997) and the Home Office advice on evaluation at that time did little to dispel confusion. 'Plausible causal mechanisms', such as those outlined below, require a detailed analysis of both the local context that CCTV is to be introduced into and the objectives that the project is designed to achieve. By keeping in mind the specific mechanisms through which CCTV can be expected to work, projects are better able to design systems that are likely to produce their desired outcomes.

- *The 'effective deployment' mechanism.* CCTV may facilitate the effective deployment of security/police officers towards areas where suspicious behaviour is occurring. They then act as a visible presence which might deter potential offenders. They may also apprehend actual offenders red-handed and disable their criminal behaviour.

- *The 'publicity (specific) mechanism'.* CCTV, and signs indicating that it is in operation, could symbolize efforts to take crime seriously and to reduce it. The potential offender may then perceive crime to be more difficult or risky and is deterred.

- *The 'appeal to the cautious' mechanism.* It might be that cautious drivers ... may use and fill those carparks with CCTV and drive out those who are more careless, whose vulnerable cars are stolen from elsewhere.
  (Examples of causal mechanisms, taken from Pawson and Tilley, 1994)

Sound theoretical reasons for the use of CCTV in tackling specific crime and disorder problems can readily be identified. However, it is noticeable that, for the most part, the staff involved with the partnerships under study adopt an extremely generalist view of the way in which CCTV 'works'. When project officers are asked why they think a CCTV scheme is beneficial for an area, a very common response is 'to reduce crime and disorder'. It has become so ingrained in crime prevention rhetoric at all levels that only a few seem to question its potential utility. This is not to say that the majority of officers blindly believe that CCTV is a panacea for crime prevention, just that the precise mechanisms by which CCTV is expected to reduce crime are not readily identified by staff responsible for project implementation.

In addition, the Home Office guidance states that 'the intervention [must be] supported by reliable evidence of its (cost-)effectiveness and sustainability, which can plausibly apply to the current crime or disorder problem'. Due to the current paucity of evidence as to the cost-effectiveness of CCTV as a crime prevention mechanism, it is reasonable that partnerships have not provided a great deal of evidence on this subject, although, to their credit, some have attempted the exercise. However, given that partnerships will be responsible for revenue costs for many years to come, the importance of this exercise should be underlined. Although at this stage in the research it is not possible to identify all the elements which make up an effective CCTV scheme, even the early observations of the implementation stage suggest that it is essential for project teams to have a clear and logical explanation as to how the cameras will be used to tackle offending, both in the short and longer term.

Consultation

The results of consultation with the residents and users of the intervention areas were submitted by most partnerships as part of the bidding process. Three main types of consultation were undertaken. The first was the Crime and Disorder Audit exercise, which contains an element of consultation used to identify areas suffering from high levels of crime and disorder. The second was consultation with users or residents' groups and associations. In addition, particularly in residential areas, project teams often undertook survey exercises that addressed, variously, respondents' levels of victimization, the fear of crime and attitudes towards the introduction of CCTV in the area. The last two types of consultation raised concerns, about both quality and consistency, which are addressed below.

Project teams often consulted with users via 'community' groups and other active bodies. This is a convenient mechanism as these groups can be called together to meet and make decisions in a way that is difficult or impossible to achieve with the entire user population. It is expedient for project teams to assume that these nominally representative groups fairly accurately reflect the views of the local population. As Edwards and Benyon point out, partnerships tend to underestimate the heterogeneity of populations and cultures in 'high-crime' areas, 'preferring instead to "imagine" such populations as a morally homogeneous community of interest' (1999, p. 14). It was not uncommon for project teams in our study to characterize the community in terms of a law-abiding majority who would support CCTV and a criminal minority that would oppose it. Any opposition to CCTV would therefore, by definition, arise from those residents with 'something to hide'. In a few cases, community or resident associations themselves provided the impetus for the bid for CCTV funding and undertook their own consultation within the residential area. However, there is nothing intrinsic to a 'community-driven' scheme that ensures all aspects of the community are involved, at least not in the examples of consultation we witnessed.

In addition to or instead of consultation with interested groups, the survey method was often used to provide evidence of support for schemes. Surveys are one-off, one-way methods of consultation and do not facilitate continued discourse with the community. In addition to this overriding concern, particular problems with the use of the survey method were common across the different projects. From fieldwork results, we know that these surveys were usually designed and carried out by agencies with a vested interest in the community saying 'yes' to CCTV installation. For example, in one case the questionnaire was written by the CCTV Action Group that was already committed to installing CCTV on the residential estate. Surveys were usually undertaken by post, which delivers a notoriously low response rate, but the lack of reliability was skated over. Surveys never contained information about the different types of CCTV schemes that could be installed nor the location or number of cameras, their capabilities and monitoring arrangements. This minimized the opportunity for respondents to make an informed choice. Indeed, respondents were usually presented only with the choice to accept or reject CCTV, rather than the opportunity to state whether they would prefer the money to be spent in another way. Respondents might prefer to spend the money on an alternative option, but accept CCTV because 'something is better than nothing'. While the Home Office funding used by the project teams was designated solely for the provision of CCTV schemes, the continued revenue funding, usually provided by the local authority for many years to come, is not.

As well as concerns about the quality of the consultation exercises undertaken by the partnerships, questions were also raised about the consistency with which users were consulted and involved. The lack of a continued relationship with users can result in a failure to fully understand their needs. More than one project team under evaluation has had to redesign a scheme, causing additional expense and delays, because it was unsatisfactory to local users. The initial consultation with users can also raise expectations of continued involvement. If this fails to materialize it can result in dissatisfaction among the users. The time at which the project goes live is a key point at which communication with residents tends to drop off rapidly. However, this is the stage when users may expect to see significant results from the CCTV cameras, and the reality of their experience may prove an anticlimax. One team experienced a steady stream of calls of complaint about the new system. They found that most of these resulted from the residents' ignorance about the way the scheme worked and a lack of knowledge amongst police control room staff of the existence and whereabouts of the new scheme. After instituting a communication exercise, they have experienced no more complaints to date.

Design and technology

A CCTV system is a technologically complex project, requiring technical expertise that is not always available among the personnel in the partnership. Where internal expertise is unavailable, it can be 'bought in' through the employment of an external consultant, although this can leave the partnership feeling vulnerable. As one project manager said, '. . . we can buy the advice, but we don't have the expertise to interrogate that advice . . .' Additionally, CCTV technology is currently undergoing revision (as may always be the case), and to schemes this appears to be a revolution. Two decisions in particular have important implications for the design of a successful scheme: the signal transfer method, and the choice between analogue or digital recording equipment. Both of these aspects of CCTV involve fast-changing technology.

The choice of signal transfer method has important cost implications, and will determine the quality of images received in the control room. For static systems the choice has largely been between fibre optic and microwave transmission, but the range of options available becomes even more complex with mobile or redeployable schemes. The introduction of wireless CCTV (open circuit television or OCTV) using the mobile-phone network as a method of data transfer has proved highly attractive to schemes seeking to deploy cameras temporarily in outlying areas. One scheme under evaluation bought this technology for use in rural or suburban areas with transient crime problems as a cost-effective means of providing temporary CCTV coverage. While the mobile nature of such a system has proved invaluable, the novelty of the technology has meant that project personnel have experienced considerable problems operating the system.

Regarding recording technology, the early starters have generally, although not exclusively, installed analogue recording systems. Those implementing later are tending to install digital recording systems. Digital technology is often seen as a good investment for the future, especially when weighed against the commonly held opinion that analogue technology will quickly be outdated. However, at the time we researched this it is often more expensive both for the hardware necessary to record footage and for storage of that footage. It is possible to combine analogue and digital recording systems; at least one of the schemes is recording footage onto DAT tapes. This will provide them with an analogue storage system with the capabilities for rapid research and review available from digital technology.

The impact of new CCTV technology has been difficult to assess at this stage in the evaluation, but thus far several key points have become apparent. Projects embracing new technology run the risk of being 'guinea pigs', making mistakes for future users to learn from. In addition, the newness of the technology can mean that there is a supplier monopoly, resulting in higher cost and reduced capacity to probe the technological advice provided.

Practical implementation

Since there were practical restrictions on the extent of research and design that could be undertaken by projects prior to receiving funding, all the projects were vulnerable to unforeseen or unpredictable practical problems during the implementation stage of the project. As these projects require a large amount of construction in public places, the involvement of independent third parties is unavoidable and this takes aspects of the implementation process out of the project teams' control. In addition, while the switch-on date is often regarded as the final stage in the process, in fact it is merely the start of what is a costly ongoing maintenance period.

During the process of implementation, projects have encountered a wide variety of practical problems that have necessitated significant alterations to original designs or costings. There were a number of examples of this: pavements in the intervention area were found not to be wide enough to install the camera pole and leave sufficient space for pedestrians; an initial survey during the winter failed to consider that foliage growth during the summer would obscure some camera viewpoints; an intervention area was nominated for heritage status, placing restrictions on the sites at which cameras could be erected; extended surveys showed that digging in one site would have to be done by hand to avoid damaging the roots of trees that were the subject of a conservation order; and a planned route for laying cabling could not be used as the digging would block off the only public access between the local station and the city centre. Many of these problems could have been better avoided had a detailed survey been carried out at the design stage; however, for most schemes the design and costing stage took place prior to the approval of funds. It is to be expected that projects were unwilling to spend large amounts of money on a detailed survey before funds for the project were guaranteed. The changes to the funding of CCTV schemes introduced by the Home Office in April 2003 may well alleviate this dilemma.

It is usual for cooperation and consent to be granted from third parties during some aspect of the project in order for implementation to progress. For example, when installing cabling, consent will commonly have to be obtained from a number of agencies including planning, heritage and health and safety departments. In some cases, the CCTV project is related to another project run by a third party and there can be 'knock-on' effects. As an example, one team was delayed because the new building in which the control room was to be housed, the construction of which was separately managed, had not been completed. In certain circumstances, suppliers of services, goods and utilities can constitute a special threat to the efficiency and cost-effectiveness of implementation. Projects can suffer from what is in effect a supplier monopoly; this takes the power out of the hands of the consumer and favours the manufacturer who is able to dictate charges.

Those few projects that have gone 'live' to date have been able to provide advice about the practical problems that they have experienced subsequent to this date. More than one project has experienced pressure to 'sign off' on the contractors' work before all the 'teething problems' have been ironed out. However, their experience suggests that this should be resisted as trivial matters can become significant when investigated further. Provision for ongoing maintenance needs to be thought through carefully. For example, one project team had a guaranteed call-out clause in their contract specifying that an engineer would visit within 24 hours of a fault being reported. Unfortunately, this was not the same as a guarantee that the problem would be fixed directly and in several cases repairs took months. The same team reported repeated problems in having to wait for parts to be ordered. Schemes involving cameras that are placed high up on buildings may experience higher maintenance costs because specialist equipment is needed to enable engineers to reach the cameras. Among partnerships with redeployable cameras, it has become clear that little consideration was initially given to the resources involved in moving cameras. For instance, the redeployment of cameras between poles requires a 'cherry picker' (a specialist vehicle for elevated working) with a trained operator, which must be available when the cameras need to be moved.

Identification of costs and resources

The funding criteria for the CCTV initiatives under the Crime Reduction Programme allowed projects to claim for capital costs, but revenue costs (e.g. funding for the ongoing monitoring, staffing and maintenance of CCTV systems) remain a local responsibility. The success of CCTV projects is dependent upon the ability to raise and sustain the necessary revenue income or to absorb costs within existing funding. The project partnerships were required to state the source of such income and that it would be sustainable for at least three years. Some funding was provided by agencies within the partnership, whether the 'lead agency' or a secondary agency. Other projects have raised funds by commercial means, for example, leasing some aspect of the system such as cabling. Some projects have raised funds from recipients, either as voluntary contributions from local businesses or through increased housing rent.

Funding supplied by the main partner agencies involved in the CCTV project is normally provided as a direct contribution to the revenue costs. To date this form of income has raised few difficulties. However, the extent to which a single agency is able to soak up unpredicted shortfalls in revenue may be critical to the future success of a project. These arise for a variety of reasons, including increased costs, unanticipated changes and the failure of other revenue streams. Once the three years of agreed funding are over, there is no guarantee that lead agency funding will still be secure if the agency's priorities change. Funding from secondary agencies may become available either through direct contributions or through the integration of more than one crime prevention project. In most cases, the availability of CCTV funding was perceived by the secondary agency as an opportunity to benefit either a project already in existence or one that has been conceived for the future.

A further source of funding has been noted in the commercial field. In some cases, particular aspects of the CCTV system such as cabling are to be leased to a local company in order to generate income for the CCTV project. Raising revenue through commercial means requires the negotiation of contracts, which is time-consuming. In one project, implementation progressed on the assumption that revenue would be obtained from the leasing out of fibre optic cabling but before any contractual agreement had been signed. Although the revenue was realized, the project took some considerable financial risk in proceeding before it was guaranteed. There is also an issue of sustainability of commercially generated funds, where the needs of the leasing or providing agency may change over time. This will become of increasing interest as the projects progress.

A third source of income is obtained from the recipients of the CCTV projects. Recipients generally include those who are assumed to benefit from the CCTV cameras, for example, residents and businesses. Two principal methods of contribution have been identified. Firstly, there is the possibility of increasing local authority housing rents, where local authorities are typically considering raising rent by approximately 50p per week for council tenants in CCTV areas. Secondly, money could be raised through contributions from local businesses within the CCTV areas, either voluntarily or via a levy. With both the above methods of raising revenue, non-contributing properties may also benefit from the CCTV project. This could cause resentment and a campaign to end charges. It may also increase the pressure for 'visible' results from the scheme, which could have a beneficial effect on the motivation of staff, or could create pressure to divert services towards those who are contributing at the expense of those who are not.

Conclusion

At this stage, in reviewing our findings to date, we may begin to draw some tentative conclusions about good practice in the future.

The activity of partnerships in the field of crime and disorder reduction extends far beyond the limits of this evaluation. However, it is of some concern to find that, while many such partnerships are relatively long established, fundamental problems still exist within their structure. An issue that has been particularly evident in the course of our fieldwork is that of accountability. In order to work together effectively, the partnership as a whole must have some method by which it can hold agencies and individuals responsible if they fail to complete tasks that they have undertaken, or honour agreements that they have made. As a corollary to this we would note, specifically, that agencies might make agreements at the strategic partnership level, but fail to ensure that the agreement is carried through to the operational level.

It is clear that in drawing up a bid, many partnerships require additional sources of expertise to draw on when gathering data as evidence, both in working with statistical data and in using surveys and other consultative methods. Although various bodies are working to improve the data sources available,[2] at present these are still subject to limitations both in quality and in the unit size at which the data can be presented. In order to improve the quality of schemes, partnerships would also benefit from a greater understanding of crime prevention measures or from access to expertise on this subject. In order to encourage partnerships to develop or seek out this expertise, future funding rounds should require much clearer explanation of the mechanisms by which CCTV or other measures are expected to work.

A number of problems were caused by the bidding process, and questions were raised about the motivation of schemes in applying for CCTV funding. In addition the time taken for bids to be approved may have resulted in changes or fluctuations in the crime problem. Finally, projects may have been reluctant to invest time and money in a detailed survey of the proposed site before funds were guaranteed, resulting in costly practical problems once installation began. However, changes to the Home Office funding practices introduced in April 2003 are expected to alleviate many of these issues.

In terms of consultation, the main concern raised was over the quality of the consultation exercises carried out. Guidance on this topic produced by the Home Office may be beneficial, and adherence to this guidance should be a requirement of any future bidding process. Ideally, involving users during the development of the bid and design should be regarded by a partnership as a key step in an ongoing process of developing a relationship with the residents in the area. It is also advised that a consultation stage, or stages, should be planned to take place once the scheme goes 'live' in order to assess that users' needs are being met and that they understand the way in which the scheme works.

With regard to practical problems of implementation, the projects under evaluation have been extremely open about the difficulties they have faced. Their main aim has been to prevent other project teams facing the problems they have encountered and to benefit from the shared experience of others. The Home Office has undertaken a series of regional seminars in an attempt to share this knowledge, and with the publication of the results of this research we hope that these aims will be achieved. At this time it is too early to tell what the impact of different types of technology will be, but we will watch with interest.

Notes

Adapted from Scarman Centre National CCTV Evaluation Team (2003) *National evaluation of CCTV early findings on scheme implementation-effective practice guide.* Home Office Development and Practice Report 7. London: Home Office (which is © Crown copyright 2003). Reproduced with permission of the Home Office.

1   The authors are contactable via Angela Spriggs, her email is: ams36@le.ac.uk. They would like to thank Gwendolyn Brandon and colleagues at the Home Office for comments on a draft of this paper; also Anthea Rose for her advice, and Matt Follett for his research input.

2   For example, the Office for National Statistics, the Police Crime Recording Agency, the Home Office, the Census Bureau, DTLR.

Bibliography

Home Office (1999) Crime and Disorder Reduction Partnership Guidance Notes. *http://www.homeoffice.gov.uk/cdact/actgch4.htm.*

Edwards, A. and Benyon, J. (1999) 'Networking and Crime at the Local Level', in Ryan, M. et al. (eds), *Criminal Justice Networks.* London: Macmillan.

Pawson, R. and Tilley, N. (1994) 'What works in evaluation research?' *British Journal of Criminology*, Vol. 34, No. 3, pp 291–307.

Pawson, R. and Tilley, N. (1997) *Realistic Evaluation.* London: Sage.

Williams, K. and Johnstone, C. (2000) 'The Politics of the Selective Gaze: Closed Circuit Television and the Policing of Public Space', *Crime, Law and Social Change*, Vol. 34, pp 183–210.

Chapter 5

Estimating the Extent, Sophistication and Legality of CCTV in London

Michael McCahill and Clive Norris [1]

Little is known about the extent of CCTV coverage in the UK. Nor do we know much about the technological and organizational capability of CCTV systems or the extent to which they comply with recent Data Protection legislation. This paper attempts to fill this gap in the existing literature by drawing on empirical research conducted on the extent, sophistication and legality of CCTV usage in publicly accessible spaces in London. The paper begins with a fictional account of CCTV in London before showing how such a scenario is increasingly mirrored in reality. To get a more precise account of the use of CCTV in publicly accessible spaces we then focus on the London borough of Wandsworth. We conclude by assessing the extent to which CCTV has become the 'fifth utility' by using our sample to extrapolate the extent of CCTV coverage in London and the country as a whole.

Introduction

While most commentators would probably agree that 'by the mid-1990s the UK had the highest density of CCTV cameras in the world',[2] there is probably less agreement over the number of surveillance cameras currently operating in this country. According to one writer, since the early 1990s over one million surveillance cameras have been installed in towns and cities across Britain, with an estimated 500 or more being added to this figure every week.[3] Nor do we know much about the technological and organizational capability of CCTV systems or the extent to which they comply with recent data protection legislation. This paper attempts to fill this gap in the existing literature by drawing on empirical research conducted on the extent, sophistication and legality of CCTV usage in publicly accessible spaces in London.[4]

Setting the scene: a fictional account of surveillance in London

It is 9.30 on a warm June morning and Claude and Helena Zidane have just touched down at London's Heathrow airport. As their plane taxis to the terminus they talk excitedly about who they might meet at the opening night party for the Tate Modern's latest exhibition. They board the travelator and head towards the baggage reclaim and are noticed by the security guard in the central CCTV control room who thinks they make a handsome middle-aged couple: he in his expensive linen suit and she in her designer label frock. This is the Zindanes' first appearance on English CCTV but it certainly will not be their last. Indeed, as they pass through baggage reclaim, on to customs and out of the airport to the Tube, they are filmed almost constantly on the 96-camera system and their images recorded for posterity on the state-of-the-art computerized digital system.[5] Rather than traipse round London with their luggage they have decided to check into their suburban hotel in Putney, south-west London, before an afternoon of sightseeing and the early evening reception and dinner.

While waiting for the train they are filmed by the cameras on the platform[6] which not only relay their images to a central control room but also to the driver of their approaching train, who in her cab has a monitor which enables her to observe the platform pictures from each station.[7] When they arrive at East Putney, they make the short walk form the platform to the exit and in the process are caught on six different cameras.[8] The two hundred-yard walk to the Putney Castle Hotel is the first time since arriving in England that they have not been filmed. However, as soon as they enter the driveway to the hotel they are picked up by the hotel's car park system and again by the lobby cameras.[9]

After a cup of coffee in their room they order a taxi to take them to town where Claude wants to take advantage of the mega-music stores on Oxford Street to top up his collection of jazz CDs and Helena wants to see if she can pick up a Gucci handbag in the sales. They are filmed getting into the cab in the hotel entrance and then their five-mile journey is monitored by a plethora of cameras watching over London's motorists. First the taxi's licence plate is recorded by one of the thousands of Traffic Master cameras which now grace Britain's roads.[10] The taxi driver is careful to observe the speed limit throughout the journey, as he does not want to be caught on the myriad of speed cameras now operated by the Metropolitan Police.[11] Similarly, he is careful to keep out of the designated bus lanes, as they are now monitored by kerbside and bus top mounted cameras.[12] On arriving at Oxford Street, they decamp and are immediately picked up on one of the 35 cameras comprising the open street CCTV system that is monitored from a control room in Marylebone police station.[13] Without exception they are recorded on the in-house CCTV system of each of the six stores they visit over the next hour and a half.[14]

It is now 1.30 and they are ready for lunch. They decide to head towards China Town in Soho to eat in a small restaurant recommended by a friend, and as they order their noodles and king prawns Helena gives Claude a small present of a silk tie. As he reaches for her hand to kiss it in thanks, he does not stop to think whether this moment of intimacy is being caught on camera. In fact it is not. The small black box pointing at them from the corner of the ceiling is in fact a dummy camera, installed by the manager as a deterrent against till snatches and handbag theft.[15] Over lunch they decide that as their legs are tired they will be lazy tourists and take a bus around the main attractions but stop off at Westminster Abbey and the British Museum. As they board the bus they are surprised to see a notice informing them that security cameras are in operation inside.[16]

At both Westminster Abbey and the British Museum their images are captured on a myriad of cameras protecting the priceless religious and cultural artefacts.[17] As they leave Westminster Abbey they walk past the Houses of Parliament which are protected by a network of over 260 cameras. It is now 5 o'clock so they decide it is time to take a taxi back to their hotel to freshen up before the evening's 7 o'clock reception. On returning to their hotel, they shower and change and order another taxi to take them up to the Tate Modern.

While they marvel at the exhibits and mingle with the famous guests they are unsurprisingly filmed on the Tate's new multi-camera system. What they had not realized was that while talking to the avant-garde performance artist Miles Monk, the tiny video cam in his hat was relaying live images of them tucking into the buffet supper directly to his website. According to the site meter 297 people were currently viewing them, as far apart as Lisbon, Los Angeles and Lagos.

When it is time to leave they decide that as it is such a pleasant evening they will stroll along the Thames back to Waterloo Station. Once inside the station they are continuously monitored by the blanket coverage of 250 CCTV cameras, part of the 1,800 cameras which cover the 16 major mainline stations in the capital. As they alight at Putney Station they are filmed on the platform and again as they exit the entrance hall of the station.[18] Before walking back to their hotel they decided to have a nightcap in the pub opposite the station. As they cross the road they are captured on the Wandsworth Borough CCTV network monitored from a centralized control room.[19] On entering the pub, Helena notices a large sign on the door announcing that the premises are under video surveillance, the purpose of the system and the name of the data controller.[20] After a quick drink they return to the hotel to sleep, although their dreams are broken by the buzz of the Metropolitan Police's video equipped helicopter which is monitoring the progress of a stolen car as it traverses south London.[21]

The reality of surveillance in London

Although we have started with a fictional account of CCTV in London it is clear that such a scenario is increasingly mirrored in reality. In what follows we first want to document the use of CCTV in a range of different settings in London to show how our fictional account increasingly mirrors the reality of routine surveillance. Next, drawing on our EU-funded study, we want to focus on the use of CCTV in one London borough in order to provide a more finely tuned and detailed account of the extent, sophistication and legality of CCTV in London.

Major infrastructure in London
London has witnessed a huge increase in the number of CCTV cameras operating in public spaces over the last decade. The catalyst for CCTV expansion in central London came in 1993 in response to the IRA's terrorist attack on Bishopgate. Following this a network of cameras was introduced to monitor the entrances to the City of London known as the 'ring of steel'. This system has now been integrated with many of the cameras operating in the City's banks and offices. 'Camerawatch', as it is known, was set up following a meeting with some 400 organizations and involves 373 systems with over 1,200 cameras.[22] The capital's busiest shopping area, Oxford Street, is also covered by a £500,000 CCTV system consisting of 35 cameras that are monitored from a centralized control room located in Marylebone police station.[23] Similarly, the Parliamentary estate is monitored by a network of 260 CCTV cameras.[24]

While there are no government records that would allow us to state the exact number of cameras in the capital, there are figures on central government funding of CCTV that give us some idea of the extent to which surveillance is becoming ubiquitous in the public spaces of the UK. Between 1994 and 1999, the four rounds of the government's CCTV Challenge Competition raised £85 million to secure the capital funding of 580 CCTV schemes, £31 million from Home Office Funds and £54 million from the partnerships. Under the Labour government's Crime Reduction Programme, between 1999 and 2001 £170 million of capital funding was available to crime and disorder reduction partnerships across the UK for new and extended public area CCTV schemes.[25]

London has done particularly well in the bidding process for centrally funded CCTV. For example, in the second round of the Crime Reduction Programme (announced on 31 March 2000) awards amounting to £79 million were made to partnerships. The successful partnerships included a total of 22 London boroughs which made bids ranging from £15,000 in the Borough of Merton to £2,718,450 in the Borough of Tower Hamlets (for improvements to the Docklands Light Railway). Between them the 22 London boroughs bid for a total of £17,883,343. This money has been used to fund new systems and to improve existing systems including 'a £1.2 million upgrade of the London Borough of Ealing's 255-camera CCTV scheme'.[26] These figures do not include other CCTV systems that have received central government funding, such as those in schools. For example, between 1997 and 2002 all 32 of the London boroughs received annual school security grants which came to a total of £13,013,510.[27]

Transport

CCTV made its first appearance on the London Underground in 1961, where five black and white cameras were installed at Holborn Station on the Central Line.[28] During the 1990s the London Underground system embarked on a programme of blanket CCTV coverage across its 250-station network. By March 1996 one company, Sony, had alone installed 5,000 cameras.[29] On the Central Line, which has 55 km of track, 34 stations and carries 166 million passengers a year, 500 CCTV cameras have been installed and are monitored by one central control room.

More recently, London Underground has introduced 85 one-man operated trains installed with a 'track to train CCTV system'. The system allows the driver to receive pictures of the platform at each station as it is approached and on arrival to see pictures of the side of the train to monitor the doors and passenger safety.[30] Meanwhile, in January 2002 the London Underground introduced 'Operation Hawkeye'—a 550-camera CCTV system designed to monitor the 58 car parks at underground stations.[31]

Limited camera surveillance has been operating on the mainline railway stations for over thirty years and like the Underground system the 1990s have seen a move towards 'blanket' CCTV coverage; Waterloo Station, for example, is estimated to have 250 cameras.[32] In 1997 a modernization programme was launched which allowed British Transport Police (BTP) full access to 1,800 CCTV cameras covering all 16 major stations in the capital.[33] In January the following year Railtrack announced a £1 billion station regeneration programme, £40 million of which is to be spent on installing CCTV and better lighting at 800 stations.[34]

Since the early 1990s speed cameras and red light enforcement cameras have increasingly been deployed on the national road network. In 1996, a survey of ten police forces found they had 102 speed cameras which were rotated between 700 sites. However, the most recent figures suggest that in London alone there are now 650 speed cameras in operation.[35] In July 1997 the Metropolitan Police announced it was to introduce an automatic licence plate recognition system in an effort to combat terrorism and violent crime.[36] This was prompted by the 'success' of a similar system launched by the City of London police in February of the same year. By integrating digital camera and computer technology, the system is capable of automatically reading vehicle number plates as they pass into the 'Square Mile' of the City of London. The numbers are then stored on computer, and matched against a database of 'suspect' or wanted vehicles. The system is capable of handling 300,000 vehicles an hour.[37]

London's motorists are also monitored by a real-time traffic information service called Trafficmaster that covers all the major roads in the capital.[38] However, the most recent expansion of cameras on the capital's roads was announced in 2002 when London's mayor, Ken Livingstone, outlined plans to introduce a traffic congestion scheme comprising 700 CCTV cameras. From 17 February 2003 motorists will have to pay £5 a day to drive into Central London between 7 am and 6.30 pm, from Monday to Friday except on public holidays. The charging zone is eight square miles and covers 1.3 per cent of the total 617 square miles of Greater London.[39]

The London Bus Lane Enforcement Camera Project also uses video cameras (mounted either on buses or at the roadside) to enforce bus lane regulations in the Metropolitan Police area. In 2000 it was estimated that the project had reached the halfway stage with some 300 bus lanes being enforced by the surveillance system.[40] By 31 March 2000, a total of 151 bus-mounted and 29 fixed cameras had been installed. Raymond Webb of the Metropolitan Police stated: 'I suspect that in a few years time, more buses will have CCTV than will not'.[41] Finally, CCTV is becoming a routine security measure inside the buses themselves. London Buses Metroline, for example (which runs 870 buses on 82 routes, carrying 162 million passengers per year), has introduced CCTV cameras on 130 buses and is now retrofitting its entire fleet.[42]

In 1996, a £600,000 digitally recorded CCTV system was installed by British Airways at Heathrow airport. The system consists of 96 cameras which capture and record video images using a video motion detection system which provides instant access to any recently recorded images and longer-term archive storage.[43] There is also extensive CCTV coverage at the entrances to the public car parks at Heathrow, Gatwick and Stanstead. These systems were introduced in the mid-1990s after it was revealed that a robbery of 1 million pounds of cash from a Heathrow airport car park was not filmed by the security cameras because all the car park's cameras were in fact dummies.[44] By early 1995 this security lapse had been remedied as the British Airports Authority installed a 100-camera system over their 18 car parks. The digital system involves a picture of each car, registration number and driver being taken on entry. The information is then stored on a remotely accessible computerized database.[45]

Cultural, tourist and leisure attractions
From our review of the security literature it would appear that the majority of the capital's major sports stadiums and arenas have extensive CCTV surveil-

lance systems. In 1998, for example, 61 cameras were installed at the former Stamford Bridge—home of Chelsea FC—ground with 'plans to increase the capability of the system to include in excess of 150 cameras in due course'.[46] On this site security officers can monitor the business activities of the stadium and the surrounding area, including the underground car park, the hotel as well as all access routes to the ground.

By conducting telephone interviews we were also able to obtain information on the CCTV systems in nine of the top cultural/tourist attractions in London. These included: the British Museum, the Natural History Museum, Kew Gardens, London Zoo, the National Gallery, the National Portrait Gallery, the Science Museum, the Tower Bridge Experience and Westminster Abbey. The size and technological sophistication of the systems varied quite considerably. The average number of cameras was 47, ranging from 11 in one institution to 140 in one of the major museums. Similarly, the annual running costs (maintenance and personnel) ranged from £6,000 to £1,000,000.

At the time of the research the nine cultural/tourist attractions had between them a total of 411 CCTV cameras. All nine institutions had CCTV systems that were monitored by CCTV operators in an on-site control room. Over three-quarters (79 per cent) of these were monitored on a continuous basis, i.e. 24 hours a day, 365 days a year. All of the systems recorded the images captured by the surveillance cameras, and four (44 per cent) of these were recorded digitally. Finally, all of the institutions had the facility to deploy security officers to events caught on camera and four (44 per cent) had installed automatic detection technologies.

Criminal justice
Although the police have been actively involved in the setting up of open-street CCTV systems throughout London, in the main, they are not the operators or owners of the systems which are normally run by the local authority. Even so, the Metropolitan Police own and control a number of mobile systems which can be temporarily deployed, particularly for public order events and increasingly their dedicated traffic enforcement cars are equipped with cameras to provide evidence of dangerous and reckless driving. However, it is inside the police station that CCTV has most proliferated. Since the early 1990s there has been a rolling programme to introduce CCTV in all custody suites throughout the Metropolitan Police area. At present coverage has been established in 32 of the 64 custody suites. Therefore within the next few years every person arrested will be subject to video recording on arrival at the police station.[47] Most recently at Kilburn police station in North London cameras have been introduced to all the cells where prisoners are detained. The initiative is specifically aimed at preventing prisoners from harming themselves while in custody and at reducing allegations of police brutality. This move is especially controversial since the

cells have integral sanitation and there is no mechanism for privacy screening of the images.[48]

CCTV is also a central feature of prison security and is used to monitor the perimeter fencing of all London prisons. However, more recently the government has actively supported the expansion of CCTV across the prison estate to combat drug dealing in prisons.[49] For example, in the London prisons of Holloway, Brixton and Wormwood Scrubs CCTV has been introduced into the visiting areas, so that all interactions between prisoners and their visitors are permanently recorded.[50]

CCTV in the Borough of Wandsworth

To get a more precise account of the use of CCTV in publicly accessible spaces we have focused on the London Borough of Wandsworth. Wandsworth is set in the heart of South London on the River Thames. It includes Balham, Battersea, Earlsfield, Putney, Roehampton, Southfields, Tooting, Wandsworth, parts of Clapham and five miles of River Thames frontage. It is the largest of the inner London boroughs, occupying an area of more than 13 square miles. The borough also has a growing population—currently some 260,000 residents.[51]

Methods
As part of the comparative work for the UrbanEye project we conducted two surveys of CCTV in Wandsworth. In the first survey we were tasked to select a street (or streets) in a busy commercial/shopping district of approximately 1.5 kilometres in length. For this purpose we chose the Upper Richmond Road from East Putney station running west to the corner of Putney High Street, and the entire length of Putney High Street. We identified 217 publicly accessible premises on these two roads. Each of the premises was visited to identify whether or not they had a CCTV system and signage notifying the public of the operation of CCTV. For those premises which were identified as having CCTV we contacted the manager and conducted a short telephone interview.

In our second survey of major commercial/civic (publicly accessible) institutions in the borough we were tasked to locate, from a list of 31 institutions,[52] the nearest example of each institution from the central point of our commercial shopping district (in this case the junction of Putney High Street and Upper Richmond Road). We then contacted the institutions and conducted telephone interviews with the managers or security managers. In total we managed to collect data on 27 of the 31 institutions.

CCTV at the borough level
In 2000 the Borough of Wandsworth had an open-street CCTV network consisting of approximately 180 cameras mainly covering town centres and housing estates.[53] Following successful bids to the Home Office's Crime Reduction Programme worth a total of £267,000, Wandsworth council intends to introduce a total of 32 new cameras to monitor the Lennox Housing Estate, St George's Hospital and the car parks in Battersea Park.[54] Meanwhile, the council recently purchased a rapid-response mobile CCTV unit that will be used in an attempt to reduce crime and anti-social behaviour. The system consists of a vehicle equipped with CCTV cameras and radios which 'will be used for both covert and overt filming purposes'.[55]

The extent of CCTV in Wandsworth
In our sample of civic/commercial institutions in Wandsworth we found:

- Out of a total of 27 public institutions 15 (56 per cent) had a CCTV system in operation.

- The hospital, public school, social welfare/benefits office, unemployment office, metro/underground, car park, shopping mall, chain store, pharmacy, bank, post office, hotel, cinema, petrol station and pub all had a CCTV system.

- However, the kindergarten, college/university, court, leisure centre, public library, church, cemetery, public toilet, small shop, restaurant, park and high-density residential area did not have CCTV systems.

- We obtained information on the number of cameras from 14 institutions. Between them these premises had a total of 127 CCTV cameras. On average there were nine cameras per institution.

Technological and organizational sophistication
We obtained information on the operation of the systems from 14 of the 15 institutions that had CCTV. While 11 of the systems (79 per cent) were monitored by observers, 5 (46 per cent) were monitored irregularly and 4 (29 per cent) did not have the facility to deploy someone to the scene of incidents caught on camera. Also, 10 (71 per cent) of the 14 institutions had fixed cameras only.

Legality of signage
To be compliant with the Data Protection Act 1998, signs have to state the purpose of the surveillance and provide contact details of the data controller so people may exercise their right to access surveillance footage relating to themselves. Our findings are listed here:

- We obtained information on signage from 13 of the 27 institutions. Nine out of 13 (69 per cent) of institutions with CCTV systems had some sort of sign declaring the presence of CCTV.

- We obtained information on the content of signs from 8 institutions. Only 2 (25 per cent) had signage in accordance with the current Data Protection Act. The other 6 institutions displayed signs that alerted the public to the operation of CCTV but failed to provide the full information legally required under the Data Protection Act.

CCTV on Putney High Street and the Upper Richmond Road
In our sample we identified 217 publicly accessible premises, of these 76 (35 per cent) were chain stores, 48 (22 per cent) were small shops and 41 (19 per cent) were eating/drinking places.

Extent of CCTV coverage

- Putney has an open-street CCTV system that is monitored from a centralized control room in Wandsworth town centre. Also, the Upper Richmond Road is monitored by several 'blue pole' cameras that are part of London's Trafficmaster network.

- In total 92 premises appeared to have cameras. However, in 6 of these cases these were 'dummy' cameras. Thus, 86 (41 per cent) out of 211 of the institutions in our sample had CCTV systems in operation. On Putney High Street 59 (49 per cent) of the institutions had CCTV in operation. On the Upper Richmond Road 18 (34 per cent) of institutions had CCTV systems.

- In the retail units in the Putney Exchange Shopping Mall a quarter (25 per cent) had CCTV in operation. However, the shopping mall itself has a 17-camera system monitored on a continuous basis (24 hours a day, 365 days a year) by security officers.

- The existence of cameras varied considerably between different institutions. For instance, while every bank in our sample had a CCTV system, none of the estate agents had a system. In contrast 6 (30 per cent) pubs/cafes, 15 (33 per cent) small shops, 8 (38 per cent) restaurants, 34 (47 per cent) of the chain stores and 3 (60 per cent) office blocks had CCTV systems.

- Our sample gained information on the number of cameras in 60 of the 86 institutions with CCTV systems. In total, there are 246 CCTV cameras in our Putney sample. The average number of cameras in these institutions is 4.1.

Technological and organizational sophistication

- We obtained information on the ownership of systems from 63 respondents, and information on the operators of systems from 62 respondents. We found that 53 (84 per cent) CCTV systems are 'in-house', and that 'in-house' staff operate 56 (90 per cent) systems.

- Forty-five out of 59 (76 per cent) institutions in our London high street have fixed cameras only.

- Forty-five out of 63 (71 per cent) institutions have one TV monitor while 2 (3 per cent) institutions have CCTV cameras but no monitor on which to view the images.

- Thirty-six out of 61 (59 per cent) institutions have the facility to split the screen on the TV monitor to display several images simultaneously, while 40 out of 58 (69 per cent) systems have sequential switching.

- Fifty-eight out of 63 (92 per cent) institutions record the images captured by their systems onto video tape and 37 out of 53 (70 per cent) systems have multiplexing. But 5 institutions do not record any images captured by the CCTV cameras.

- In 13 out of 62 (21 per cent) of those institutions with CCTV systems the images displayed on the monitors are not routinely observed by security or staff.

- Thirty-six out of 50 (72 per cent) systems are monitored by a single person, 38 out of 49 (78 per cent) are monitored 'irregularly', while only 5 (10 per cent) systems are monitored on a continuous basis (i.e. 24 hours a day/7 days a week).

- In 40 out of 49 (82 per cent) institutions those monitoring the system have other tasks to carry out.

- In terms of system integration, only 2 (3 per cent) institutions have the facility to relay pictures captured by their system to an outside institution (i.e. the police). However, 18 (29 per cent) have electronic communication links (e.g. radio links and panic alarms) with other police/security systems.

- Only 3 out of 61 (5 per cent) institutions have automatic detection technology, while 23 out of 62 (37 per cent) are unable to deploy someone to the scene to deal with incidents caught on camera.

Legality of signage

- Only 43 (53 per cent) out of a total of 81 premises with CCTV displayed a sign declaring the operation of CCTV.

- We obtained information on the content of signs from 46 premises. Only 10 (22 per cent) had signage in accordance with data protection law. At the other 36 (78 per cent) premises, although there were signs, they failed to provide the full information legally required under the Data Protection Act.

Conclusion: CCTV as the fifth utility?

Writing in 1996, Steven Graham argued that CCTV was set to become the 'fifth utility'.[56] He reminded us that the classic utilities which provide water, waste, energy and telecommunications developed from the local, piecemeal and patchy provision in the nineteenth century to become, during the twentieth century, near universal in coverage, standardized technologically, nationally regulated and dominated by a few key service providers. We would like to conclude by assessing the extent to which CCTV has become the 'fifth utility' by using our sample to extrapolate the extent of CCTV coverage in London to the country as a whole.

We can see from our Putney sample that 41 per cent of premises had CCTV systems in operation and that these were augmented by the open-street and traffic surveillance systems. In our sample the average number of cameras per institution with CCTV was 4.1. If we begin by assuming that the extent of CCTV coverage in Putney is broadly representative of CCTV coverage across the whole of London, we can estimate that 41 per cent (102,910) of the 251,000 businesses registered for VAT in London would have a CCTV system. Between them these businesses will have 421,931 surveillance cameras. If we add to these the number of surveillance cameras operating in other public institutions (open-street systems, transport, hospital, schools, etc.) it would not be unreasonable to 'guestimate' that Londoners are monitored by at least 500,000 CCTV cameras. This means that in London (with a population of 7.2 million residents) there is approximately one camera for every 14 people. From these figures we would suggest that in the UK (with a population of almost 60 million) there are at least 4,285,000 surveillance cameras in operation. In terms of universality it would indeed appear that, as Steven Graham predicted in 1996, in the intervening years CCTV has indeed moved much closer to becoming a 'fifth utility'.

However, while the extent of CCTV coverage has exponentially increased over the last decade, it is clear that many of the systems are small operations with very little technological or organizational sophistication. For instance, the vast majority are in-house systems monitored by in-house staff, often one person scanning a single monitor on an irregular basis because they have a host of other duties to attend to. Moreover, very few systems have the capacity to relay the images to another organization such as the police, and one-third have no capacity to deploy someone to the scene to deal with incidents caught on camera. If ubiquity is the first condition of CCTV becoming a 'fifth utility' there is still a long way to go before systems at the local level become standardized and centralized under the direction of a few major service providers.

Finally, as Graham noted, a key element marking the development of the classic utilities was the move from local, piecemeal control to national statutory regulation. With the passing of the new Data Protection Act in 1998, the absence of legislative control that characterized the initial growth of CCTV in Britain has been rectified. However, from our data it would appear that the Act has been more symbolic than real in its effects. In terms of the legality of CCTV systems, we found that just over half (53 per cent) of institutions with CCTV systems in our Putney sample had signage. However, we found that the majority of these signs were not in accordance with the law as stated in the Data Protection Act 1998. Many of the signs, for example, were not 'clearly visible and legible to members of the public', did not have adequate specification of the data controller (i.e. identity of the person/organization responsible for the scheme and contact details), and did not give details of the purpose of the scheme.[57] Based on these criteria we found that less than one-quarter (22 per cent) of the signs in our sample were in accordance with the law. If these figures are an accurate reflection of the legality of CCTV systems in the capital's major businesses, it would mean that 80,269 (78 per cent) of the CCTV systems in London's business space are not compliant with the Data Protection Act.

Notes

1   Michael McCahill is a full-time researcher in the Department of Contemporary and Applied Social Sciences at the University of Hull; tel.: 01482 465715; e-mail: M.McCahill@hull.ac.uk. Clive Norris is Professor of Sociology at the University of Sheffield; tel.: 0114 222 6460; e-mail: C.Norris@sheffield.ac.uk. The authors gratefully acknowledge financial and research support from the European Commission's Fifth Framework RTD Project on surveillance entitled UrbanEye.

2   Muncie, J. (2001) 'Surveillance', in McLaughlin, E. and Muncie, J. (eds), *The Sage Dictionary of Criminology*. London: Sage.

3   *Sunday Times*, 14 February 2002.

4   This paper is based on findings from our EU funded UrbanEye research which forms part of a three-year comparative project on the use of CCTV surveillance technology in seven European capital cities. Contract no. HPSE-CT2001-00094. Further details can be found at: *http://www.urbaneye.net/*.

5   *CCTV Today*, July 1996, p 34.

6   Since the early 1990s the London Underground has embarked on installing cameras throughout their stations and platforms and there is now almost blanket coverage of all stations.

7   In 1995 London Underground introduced their first 'track to train CCTV system' (*CCTV Today*, November 1995).

8   Based on first-hand observation from our fieldwork.

9   Based on first-hand observation from our fieldwork.

10   See *http://www.trafficmaster.co.uk* for details of this system.

11   *Sunday Times*, 27 February 2002.

12   There is an ongoing programme of CCTV installation to cover all of London's bus lanes—currently over half are now monitored by 170 cameras. See *CCTV Today*, 2001, p 4.

13   Unusually the Oxford Street system is run and monitored by the police directly. All other high-street and town-centre systems covering the main shopping areas of London are operated and run by the local authority in partnership with the police. [From interview data.]

14   From our sample in Putney High Street nearly half of the chain stores had CCTV. However, given the importance of Oxford Street as the premier shopping street of the capital and its attraction to shoplifters and pickpockets it is not unreasonable to assume that all the major stores on this street have CCTV.

15   In our sample several premises had dummy cameras and although they are not filmed here, if they had eaten in the restaurant next door, there would be a high chance that their moment of intimacy would have been filmed: from our sample around 40 per cent of restaurants had cameras.

16   See *http://www.londontransport.co.uk*.

17   Our research shows that nearly all the major tourist attractions, galleries and museums in London are protected by CCTV.

18   Based on first-hand observation from our fieldwork.

19   All of Wandsworth's town centres are monitored on the council's 180 borough-wide camera network.

20   Based on first-hand observation from our fieldwork.

21   See *http://www.timeforcitizenship.com/police/about_prevent.asp* for details of the Metropolitan Police's Air Support Arm.

22   *CCTV Today*, November 1995, p 28.

23   *CCTV Today*, 1997, p 3.

24   POST (Parliamentary Office of Science and Technology) (2000) 'CCTV', No. 175, at *http://www.parliament.uk/post/home.htm*.

25   Hansard (2000) *House of Commons Written Answers for 18 January (pt. 4)*, at *http://www.parliament.the-stationary-of . . . 900/cmhansrd/vo000118/text/ 00118w04.html.*

26   *CCTV Today* (2002), 'Ealing Control Room Dismantles Video Wall', January– February, p 4.

27   DfEE (2001) *School Security*, at: *http://www.dfee.gov.uk/schoolsecurity/alloctions. shtml.*

28   *CCTV Today*, November 1996, p 10.

29   *CCTV Today*, March 1996, p 35.

30   *CCTV Today*, November 1995.

31   *CCTV Today*, March/April 2002, p 5.

32   *Professional Security*, March 2002, p 31.

33   *CCTV Today*, September 1997, p 4.

34   *CCTV Today*, September 1997; January 1998.

35   *Sunday Times*, 27 February 2002.

36   *Independent*, 22 July 1997.

37   Norris, C. and Armstrong, G. (1999) *The Maximum Surveillance Society*, Oxford: Berg, p 45.

38   See *http://www.trafficmaster.co.uk.*

39   *The Times*, 27 February 2002, p 10.

40   Hansard (2000) *House of Commons Written Answers for 25 July (pt. 7)*, at *http://www.parliament.the-stationary-of . . . 900/cmhansrd/vo000725/text/ 00725w07.html.*

41   *CCTV Today*, May 2001, p 4.

42   London Transport (2002) 'North West London Bus Garage Hosts Golden Jubilee Royal Visit', release 6 June 2002, located at *http://www.londontransport. co.uk/press_414.shtml*; accessed 12 June 2002.

43   *CCTV Today*, July 1996, p 34.

44   *Guardian*, 3 April 1994.

45   *CCTV Today*, March 1996, pp 10–14, in Norris and Armstrong, op. cit., p 46.

46   *CCTV Today*, March 2000, p 44.

47   Metropolitan Police (2001) *Custody Suite CCTV Policy (December 2001)*, located at *http://www.met.police.uk/publications/special_notice_20-01.htm*; accessed 12 June 2002.

48   Newburn, T. and Hayman. S (2001) *Policing, Surveillance and Social Control: CCTV and Police Monitoring of Suspects.* Cullompton: Willan Publishing.

49   Home Office (2000) *Government reply to the Fifth Report from the Home Affairs Committee Session 1998–9 Drugs in Prison*, located at *http://www.parliament. the-stationery:office.co.uk/cgibin/htm_hl?DB = ukparl&STEMMER = en&WORDS = drug + prison + &COLOUR = Red&STYLE = &URL = /pa/ cm200001/cmselect/cmhaff/248/24814.htm#muscat_highlighter_first_match.*

50   HMIP (2001) *Report on and Unannounced Follow-up Inspection of HM Prison Wormword Scrubs 7–17 February 2000*, located at *http://www.homeoffice.gov.uk/ hmipris/insrep.htm#Full Announced Inspections*; accessed 12 June 2002.

51   *Wandsworth Fact File* (2001) Wandsworth City Council: Economic Development Office.

52   The institutions included a hospital, public school, benefits office, unemployment office, metro/underground, car park, shopping mall, chain store, pharmacy, bank, post office, hotel, cinema, petrol station, public house, kindergarten, college/university, court, leisure centre, public library, church, cemetery, public toilet, small shop, restaurant, park and high-density residential area.

53   Wandsworth Council Press Release (2000) 'New Boost in Fight against Burglaries', 10 April.

54   Wandsworth Council Press Release (2000) 'Crime Cameras Boost for Lennox Estate', 20 March.

55   Wandsworth Council Press Release (2000) 'Mobile Crime Cameras Take to the Road', 13 June.

56   See Graham, S., Brooks, J. and Heery, D. (1996) Towns on the Television: Closed Circuit TV in British Towns and Cities, *Local Government Studies*, Vol. 22, No. 3, pp 3–27, and Graham, S. (1998) 'Towards the Fifth Utility? On the Extension and Normalisation of Public CCTV', in Norris C., Moran J. and Armstrong G. (eds), *Surveillance, Closed Circuit Television and Social Control*. Aldershot: Ashgate.

57   Data Protection Act 1998: CCTV Codes of Practice, 'siting the cameras', paragraphs 8–12. Located at *http://www.dataprotection.gov.uk*. Accessed May 12 2003.

Chapter 6

How to Evaluate the Impact of CCTV on Crime

David P. Farrington and Kate A. Painter[1]

The main aim of this paper is to specify how researchers could carry out high-quality evaluations of the effect of CCTV on crime rates. Five criteria of methodological quality are described: statistical conclusion validity, internal validity, construct validity, external validity and descriptive validity. The quality of CCTV evaluations can be assessed using the Maryland scientific methods scale. The minimum acceptable evaluation design is to have before and after measures of crime in experimental and comparable control areas. Desirable features of future evaluations include using several experimental and control areas, conducting a randomized experiment, carrying out surveys of potential victims and potential offenders, having a long time series of crime rates before and after CCTV, measuring displacement and diffusion of benefits by using adjacent and non-adjacent control areas, testing hypotheses about mediators and moderators, carefully measuring features of the CCTV scheme and features of persons and settings, having independent evaluators and carrying out cost-benefit analysis.

Introduction

It seems possible that more than £1,000 million has been spent on CCTV schemes so far in the UK.[2] It also seems possible that CCTV is more widely used in the UK than in any other country. The key question is whether—in order to reduce crime—it is most cost-effective to spend £1,000 million of taxpayers' money on CCTV or whether this would be better spent on more police officers, more prison cells, more cognitive-behavioural programmes for offenders, more pre-school intellectual enrichment programmes, more restorative justice programmes, better street lighting, more community regeneration programmes, and so on.[3]

In order to answer this question, high-quality evaluation research is needed on CCTV and on other interventions intended to reduce crime. Too many past evaluations have been 'quick and dirty'. As taxpayers, we need high-quality evaluation research that is convincing and will hold up in the face of criticism. Fortunately, the research on CCTV currently being funded by the Home Office and carried out by Professor Martin Gill and his colleagues at Leicester University promises to be the best ever conducted on this topic in the UK.

The main aim of this article is to specify how a researcher should attempt to investigate the effects of CCTV on crime rates. There are many other questions about CCTV that we do not address, including technical features of the systems (e.g. the clarity of the pictures), the ability of CCTV to detect offenders, the use of CCTV pictures as evidence by the police, CCTV as an aid to police deployment or officer safety, the likelihood and speed of police responses to events shown on CCTV, civil liberties issues, and effects of CCTV on fear of crime.

Previous evaluations
Previous evaluations of the effects of CCTV on crime rates reviewed by Welsh and Farrington[4] have often been flawed for a variety of reasons. Some have only studied the effects of CCTV on crime in an experimental area, with no comparable control area. Hence, it is difficult to know how far any decrease in crime in the experimental area should be attributed to CCTV as opposed to numerous other possibilities, or even whether it merely reflects national trends. Other studies have had insufficient statistical power to detect any effect of CCTV because of the small number of crimes committed before CCTV was introduced. Most evaluations have relied on official record measures of crime, making it impossible to determine how far CCTV caused an increase—or even a decrease—in police recording. Few evaluations included surveys of potential victims or potential offenders in order to test hypotheses about mediators between CCTV and crime, for example whether CCTV deterred potential offenders or encouraged potential victims to take more precautions against crime. Also, it is important to establish how far potential offenders and potential victims knew about the existence of a CCTV scheme.

Another problem of previous studies is that they have rarely presented a long time series of crimes in experimental and control areas before and after CCTV. This would be useful in investigating how far a decrease in crime reflected regression to the mean. This can occur when an intervention is introduced just after an unusually high crime rate in an area, which is likely to be followed by a decrease in crime because of normal fluctuations. Also, a long time series of crimes would make it possible to study the persistence of any crime-reducing effects or the extent to which they wore off quickly.

In many evaluations, CCTV is confounded with other interventions such as improved street lighting, making it difficult to disentangle the specific effects of CCTV. Also, studies rarely have had adequate measures of effect size or adequate tests of the statistical significance of any effect on crime. It is important to have a quantitative measure of how much crime is reduced by CCTV. There has been no attempt to document a dose–response relationship between the intensity or coverage of CCTV, or other features of CCTV schemes, and the amount of reduction in crime, and hardly any comparisons of the financial costs and benefits of CCTV. It is important to estimate how many pounds are saved, or how many crimes are saved, for every pound expended on CCTV.[5]

In general, studies have not attempted to assess moderators[6] of any effect of CCTV, such as characteristics of residents or different areas that might influence the strength of any effect. The systematic review by Welsh and Farrington found that crimes decreased more in car parks than in city centres or public transport settings, but it is unclear how far this was because CCTV was confounded with other interventions in car park evaluations.[7] Also, there has been little attempt to measure displacement of crime from experimental areas to other places or the diffusion of the benefits of CCTV to adjacent areas. Finally, many evaluations have been carried out by researchers with a personal stake in the results, raising the issue of how far these evaluations are truly unbiased and independent. Some past evaluators (or their funding agencies) have been highly motivated to prove that CCTV caused a decrease in crime.

Methodological quality criteria

A great deal is known about how to maximize methodological quality in evaluation research. According to Cook and Campbell,[8] methodological quality depends on four criteria: statistical conclusion validity, internal validity, construct validity and external validity. 'Validity' here refers to the correctness of inferences about cause and effect, for example about the effects of CCTV on crime.

From the time of John Stuart Mill, the main criteria for establishing a causal relationship have been that (a) the cause precedes the effect—here, the introduction of CCTV precedes the decrease in crime; (b) the cause is related to the effect—CCTV is associated with a decrease in crime; and (c) other plausible alternative explanations of the effect can be excluded—this is the main challenge to evaluators. The main aim of the Campbell validity typology is to identify plausible alternative explanations (threats to valid causal inference) so that researchers can anticipate likely criticisms of their conclusions and design evaluation studies to answer them. If threats to valid causal inference cannot be ruled out in the design, they should at least be measured and their importance estimated.

Following Lösel and Koferl,[9] we have added descriptive validity, or the adequacy of reporting, as a fifth criterion of the methodological quality of evaluation research. This is because, in order to complete a systematic review of the evidence on the effect of CCTV on crime, it is important that information about key features of the evaluation is provided in each research report. It is surprising how often reports do not provide key information about such topics as characteristics of residents and areas (especially control areas) and numbers of crimes committed in different time periods.

Statistical conclusion validity

Statistical conclusion validity is concerned with whether the presumed cause and the presumed effect (crime rates) are related. Measures of effect size and their associated confidence intervals should be calculated. In their systematic review, Welsh and Farrington[10] used the percentage change in crime in a control area compared with an experimental area as their main measure of effect size. Over all evaluation studies, CCTV was followed by a small decrease in crime in experimental areas compared with control areas. Statistical significance (the probability of obtaining the observed effect size if the null hypothesis of no relationship were true) should also be calculated, but in many ways it is less important than the effect size. This is because a statistically significant result could indicate a large effect in a small sample or a small effect in a large sample, or—in the case of CCTV—a large change in a low crime rate or a small change in a high crime rate.

The main threats to statistical conclusion validity are insufficient statistical power to detect the effect (e.g. because of small sample size or—here—small numbers of crimes committed before the intervention) and the use of inappropriate statistical techniques (e.g. where the data violate the underlying assumptions of a statistical test). Statistical power refers to the probability of correctly rejecting the null hypothesis when it is false, or correctly detecting the effect of CCTV on crime. Other threats to statistical conclusion validity include the use of many statistical tests (in a so-called 'fishing expedition' for significant results) and the heterogeneity of the experimental units (e.g. the people or areas in experimental and control conditions). The more variability there is in the units, the harder it will be to detect any effect of the intervention.

Internal validity

Internal validity refers to the correctness of the key question about whether the intervention—CCTV—really did cause a change in the outcome—crime—and it has generally been regarded as the most important type of validity.[11] In investigating this question, some kind of comparable control condition is essential in order to estimate what would have happened to the experimental units (e.g. people or areas) if the intervention had not been applied to them—termed the 'counterfactual inference'. Experimental control is usually better than statistical control. One problem is that the control areas rarely receive no treatment, but instead typically receive the more usual treatment or some kind of treatment that is different from the experimental intervention. Therefore, it is important to specify the effect size of CCTV 'compared to what?'

The main threats to internal validity are as follows:[12]

- *Selection.* The effect—here, the change in the crime rate—reflects pre-existing differences between experimental and control conditions. For example, crime may have decreased in the experimental area not because of CCTV but because of some other pre-existing feature of that area.

- *History.* The effect is caused by some event occurring at the same time as the intervention, for example changed police practices or a new community programme. CCTV is often installed in high-crime areas where there are other concurrent initiatives.

- *Maturation/trends.* The effect reflects a continuation of pre-existing trends, e.g. in normal human development in studies of individuals, or in crime rates in studies of areas. For example, crime steadily decreased in England and Wales in the second half of the 1990s.[13]

- *Instrumentation.* The effect is caused by a change in the method of measuring the outcome, for example a change in police recording practices in the experimental area.

- *Testing.* The pre-test measurement causes a change in the post-test measure. For example, participating in a before victim survey may affect responses in an after victim survey.

- *Regression to the mean.* Where an intervention is implemented on units with unusually high scores (e.g. areas with high crime rates), natural fluctuation will cause a decrease in these scores on the post-test which may be mistakenly interpreted as an effect of the intervention—CCTV. The opposite (an increase) happens when interventions are applied to low crime rate areas or low scoring people, but this is uncommon. Generally, the Home Office will only fund CCTV in high crime areas.

- *Differential attrition.* The effect is caused by differential loss of units (e.g. people) from experimental compared to control conditions. For example, this might explain changes in victim survey results.

- *Causal order.* It is unclear whether the intervention preceded the outcome. It is important to document when a CCTV scheme becomes operational, which may be spread over a long time period.

In addition, there may be interactive effects of threats. For example, a selection-maturation effect may occur if the experimental and control conditions have different pre-existing trends, or a selection-history effect may occur if the experimental and control conditions experience different historical events (e.g. where they are located in different settings).

In principle, a randomized experiment has the highest possible internal validity because it can rule out all these threats. For example, a large number of city blocks could be assigned at random either to have CCTV coverage or not. However, no randomized experiment has ever been carried out to evaluate the effects of CCTV on crime rates. Randomization is the only method of assignment that controls for *unknown* and *unmeasured* confounders as well as those that are known and measured.

The conclusion that the intervention—CCTV—really did cause a change in the outcome—crime—is not necessarily the final conclusion. It is desirable to go beyond this and investigate links in the causal chain between CCTV and crime ('mediators' according to Baron and Kenny[14]), the dose–response relationship between CCTV features and crime, and the validity of any theory linking CCTV and crime.

Construct validity
Construct validity refers to the adequacy of the operational definition and measurement of the theoretical constructs that underlie the intervention and the outcome. For example, if a project aims to investigate the effect of surveillance on offending, did CCTV really increase surveillance? Whereas the operational definition and measurement of physical constructs such as height and weight are not contentious, this is not true of most criminological constructs.

The main threats to construct validity centre on the extent to which the intervention succeeded in changing what it was intended to change (e.g. how far there was treatment fidelity or implementation failure) and on the validity and reliability of outcome measures (e.g. how adequately police-recorded crime rates reflect true crime rates). It is often challenging to carry out victim surveys in city centres, public transport settings or car parks, because there is no convenient population list of people at risk from which to draw a sample. The degree of implementation of the CCTV scheme needs to be investigated in a process evaluation. Key features of a CCTV scheme (e.g. the quality of the operators) need to be classified and related to effect size measures. Displacement of offending and 'diffusion of benefits' of the intervention should also be investigated.[15]

Other threats to construct validity include those arising from the effects of a participant's knowledge of the intervention and problems of contamination of treatment (e.g. where the control area receives elements of the intervention). Whereas double-blind trials are advocated in medicine, it seems likely that the public needs to know about CCTV for it to have any effect. It is also desirable to investigate interaction effects between different interventions or different ingredients of an intervention. For example, CCTV combined with improved street lighting may have a disproportionally bigger effect on crime rates than either alone.

External validity
External validity refers to the generalizability of causal relationships across different persons, places, times and operational definitions of interventions and outcomes (for example from a demonstration project to the routine large-scale application of an intervention). It is difficult to investigate this within one evaluation study, unless it is a large-scale multi-site trial such as that being carried out by Professor Martin Gill and his colleagues. External validity can be established more convincingly in systematic reviews and meta-analyses of numerous evaluation studies.

The main threats to external validity listed by Shadish et al.[16] consist of interactions of causal relationships (effect sizes) with types of persons, settings, interventions and outcomes. For example, an intervention designed to reduce crime may be effective with some types of people and in some types of places but not in others. A key issue is whether the effect size varies according to whether those who carried out the research had some kind of stake in the results (e.g. if a project is funded by a government agency, the agency may be embarrassed if the evaluation shows no effect of its highly-trumpeted intervention). There may be boundary conditions within which interventions do or do not work, or moderators of a causal relationship in the terminology of Baron and Kenny.[17] As mentioned, CCTV may work better in car parks than in other settings. It is important to measure features of persons and settings that might influence the effects of CCTV. Also, mediators of causal relationships (links in the causal chain) may apply in some settings but not in others. Ideally, theories should be proposed to explain these kinds of interactions.

Descriptive validity
Descriptive validity refers to the adequacy of the presentation of key features of an evaluation in a research report. As mentioned, systematic reviews can only be carried out satisfactorily if the original evaluation reports document key data on issues such as the number of participants, features of areas and the effect size. A list of minimum elements to be included in an evaluation report would include at least the following:

- Design of the study: how were experimental units (e.g. areas) allocated to experimental or control conditions?

- Characteristics of experimental units and settings (e.g. age and gender of individuals, socio-demographic features of areas). How far were experimental and control areas comparable?

- Sample sizes and attrition rates (e.g. in surveys).

- Causal hypotheses to be tested, and theories from which they are derived.

- The operational definition and detailed description of the intervention (including its intensity and duration). It is important to report key features of CCTV schemes such as their coverage and whether they are actively monitored.

- Implementation details and programme delivery personnel.

- Description of what interventions the control condition received.

- The operational definition and measurement of the outcome, before and after the intervention. Ideally, both official record and victim survey measures of crime should be used, and preferably also self-reported offending measures.

- The reliability and validity of outcome measures.

- The follow-up period after the intervention. Ideally, this should be long enough to investigate the persistence of effects.

- Effect size, confidence intervals, statistical significance, statistical methods used. Ideally, a cost-benefit analysis should be carried out.

- How independent and extraneous variables were controlled so that it was possible to disentangle the impact of the intervention, or how threats to internal validity were ruled out.

- Who knows what about the intervention.

- Conflict of interest issues: who funded the intervention and how independent were the researchers?

It would be desirable for professional associations, funding agencies, journal editors and/or the Campbell Collaboration[18] to get together to develop a checklist of items that must be included in all research reports on impact evaluations.

The Maryland Scientific Methods Scale

It is often valuable to use a scale to assess the methodological quality of evaluations, and the most influential methodological quality scale in criminology is the Maryland Scientific Methods Scale (SMS). This was developed for use in large-scale reviews of what works or does not work in preventing crime.[19] The main aim of the SMS is to communicate to scholars, policy-makers and practitioners in the simplest possible way that studies evaluating the effects of criminological interventions differ in methodological quality. Hence, a simple five-point scale was used rather than a summation of scores (e.g. from 0 to 100) on a number of specific criteria. It was intended that each point on the scale should be understandable, and the scale is as follows:

Level 1 Correlation between a prevention programme and a measure of crime at one point in time (e.g. 'areas with CCTV have lower crime rates than areas without CCTV').

This design fails to rule out many threats to internal validity and also fails to establish causal order.

Level 2 Measures of crime before and after the programme, with no comparable control condition (e.g. 'crime decreased after CCTV was installed in an area').

This is one of the most common evaluation designs but it is flawed. It establishes causal order but fails to rule out many threats to internal validity. Level 1 and Level 2 designs were considered inadequate and uninterpretable by Cook and Campbell.[20]

Level 3 Measures of crime before and after the programme in experimental and comparable control conditions (e.g. 'crime decreased after CCTV was installed in an experimental area, but there was no decrease in crime in a comparable control area').

As mentioned, this was considered to be the minimum interpretable design by Cook and Campbell,[21] and it is also regarded as the minimum design that is adequate for drawing conclusions about what works in the book *Evidence-Based Crime Prevention*.[22] It can rule out many threats to internal validity, including history, maturation/trends, instrumentation, testing effects and differential attrition. The main problems with it centre on selection effects and regression to the mean (because of the non-equivalence of the experimental and control areas).

Level 4 Measures of crime before and after the programme in multiple experimental and control units, controlling for other variables that influence crime (e.g. 'victimization of areas under CCTV surveillance decreased compared to victimization of control areas, after controlling for features of areas that influenced their victimization').

This design has better statistical control of extraneous influences on the outcome and hence deals with selection and regression threats more adequately.

Level 5 Random assignment of programme and control conditions to units (e.g. 'victimization of areas randomly assigned to have CCTV surveillance decreased compared to victimization of control areas').

Providing that a sufficiently large number of areas are randomly assigned, those in the experimental condition will be equivalent (within the limits of statistical fluctuation) to those in the control condition on all possible extraneous variables that influence the outcome of crime. Hence, this design deals with selection and regression problems and has the highest possible internal validity.

Conclusions

The minimum acceptable evaluation design is to have before and after measures of crime in experimental and comparable control areas. It is desirable in future evaluations of the effects of CCTV on crime rates to compare several experimental areas with several comparable control areas. If the areas were relatively small, it might be possible to randomly allocate areas to experimental or control conditions or to have alternate periods with or without CCTV coverage (e.g. using mobile cameras). In addition, future evaluations should include interviews with potential offenders and potential victims to find out what they know about the CCTV scheme, to test hypotheses about mediators between CCTV and crime, and to have measures of crime other than those from official sources. It would be desirable to have a long time series of crime rates before and after CCTV to investigate regression to the mean and the persistence of any effects on crime. Also, it is important to disentangle the effects of CCTV from the effects of other interventions such as improved street lighting. For example, an experiment could include four conditions in a Latin Square design: CCTV plus improved lighting, CCTV alone, improved lighting alone, and neither.

In planning an evaluation, it is important to ensure that there is sufficient statistical power to detect any effect of CCTV on crime. In other words, the number of crimes in each condition before the intervention should be substantial. Also, effects should be measured for different types of crimes. CCTV might be expected to influence outdoor crimes more than indoor crimes, for example. Displacement and diffusion of benefits should be studied by comparing experimental areas with adjacent and non-adjacent control areas. If crime decreased in an experimental area, increased in an adjacent control area and stayed constant or decreased in a non-adjacent control area, this might be evidence of displacement. If crime decreased in an experimental area and in an adjacent control area but stayed constant or increased in a non-adjacent control area, this might be evidence of diffusion of benefits.

Hypotheses about moderators should be tested by classifying types of areas and types of people living in them and seeing how these factors were related to the effect of CCTV on crime. It is important to monitor changes in CCTV over time and any implementation problems, as well as changes in other factors in the areas that might influence crime. The intensity of CCTV coverage and other features of CCTV schemes (e.g. the probability of police responding to incidents seen on CCTV) should be assessed to investigate if there is a dose–response relationship between these features and the effect size. The amount of publicity about the CCTV scheme should be documented.

The effect size, confidence intervals and statistical significance should be calculated. The most meaningful effect size measure is the change in crime in an experimental area compared with a control area. In studying the effect of CCTV on crime, regression analyses can be carried out that control for prior crimes and for individual and community factors that influence crime. Cost-benefit analyses should be conducted to assess if the financial benefits of CCTV outweigh its financial costs, and how CCTV compares with other interventions in the cost of reducing crimes. Ideally, the evaluators of CCTV programmes should be independent of the implementers and funders and should have no stake in the outcome of the evaluation. At a minimum, any possible conflict of interest should be declared.

One of the greatest challenges facing evaluators is that CCTV has become so widespread that it may be difficult to find a control area without CCTV. One possible solution to this would be to have a control area that has a constant level of CCTV both before and after it is introduced in an experimental area. Alternatively, the effect of withdrawing CCTV from an area could be investigated in principle (although this may be unpopular with residents!). Another possible solution would be to compare small areas covered by CCTV within an experimental area with small areas not covered, since CCTV typically does not cover every inch of an experimental area.

Undoubtedly, the quality of CCTV has increased enormously over the years, and it may be that future schemes will be more effective in reducing crime than past ones. The challenge to researchers is to ensure that the quality of their evaluations also increases commensurably, so that their results can remain convincing and can withstand criticisms from evaluation specialists.

Notes

1   David P. Farrington is Professor of Psychological Criminology and Kate A. Painter is Senior Research Associate at the Institute of Criminology, Cambridge University, 7 West Road, Cambridge CB3 9DT. E-mails: dpf1@cam.ac.uk; Kate.Painter@ntlworld.com. We are very grateful to Maureen Brown for excellent word processing. This paper was given at a conference on 'Evaluating the Real Evidence on CCTV' in Leicester in November 2002.

2   Between 1999 and 2001, £170 million was spent by the Home Office on CCTV schemes: see p 8 of Home Office Policing and Reducing Crime Unit (2001)

Invitation to Tender: Evaluation of CCTV Initiatives. London: Home Office (21 March). In previous years (1996–98), CCTV accounted for more than three-quarters of total spending on crime prevention by the Home Office: see Koch, B.C.M. (1998) *The Politics of Crime Prevention.* Aldershot: Ashgate, p 49. CCTV schemes are also funded by other central and local government agencies.

3   See Sherman, L.W., Farrington, D.P., Welsh, B.C. and MacKenzie, D.L. (eds) (2002) *Evidence-Based Crime Prevention.* London: Routledge.

4   Welsh, B.C. and Farrington, D.P. (2002) *Crime Prevention Effects of Closed Circuit Television: A Systematic Review.* Home Office Research Study No. 252. London: Home Office.

5   See Welsh, B.C., Farrington, D.P. and Sherman, L.W. (eds) (2001) *Costs and Benefits of Preventing Crime.* Boulder, CO: Westview.

6   For a discussion of mediators and moderators, see Baron, R.M. and Kenny, D.A. (1986) The Moderator-Mediator Variable Distinction in Social Psychology Research: Conceptual, Strategic and Statistical Considerations, *Journal of Personality and Social Psychology*, Vol. 51, pp 1173–82.

7   Welsh and Farrington, op. cit. CCTV was generally not confounded with other interventions in city centre evaluations.

8   Cook, T.D. and Campbell, D.T. (1979) *Quasi-Experimentation: Design and Analysis Issues for Field Settings.* Chicago: Rand McNally. See also Shadish, W.R., Cook, T.D. and Campbell, D.T. (2002) *Experimental and Quasi-Experimental Designs for Generalized Causal Inference.* Boston: Houghton-Mifflin.

9   Lösel, F. and Koferl, P. (1989) Evaluation Research on Correctional Treatment in West Germany: A Meta-Analysis, in Wegener, H., Lösel, F. and Haisch, J. (eds), *Criminal Behaviour and the Justice System: Psychological Perspectives.* New York: Springer-Verlag. See also Farrington, D.P. (2003) Methodological Quality Standards for Evaluation Research, *Annals of the American Academy of Political and Social Science*, Vol. 587, pp 49–68.

10   Welsh and Farrington, op. cit

11   Shadish et al., op. cit., p 97.

12   Ibid., p 55.

13   Home Office (2001) *Criminal Statistics, England and Wales, 2000*, Cmnd 5312. London: Stationery Office, p 27.

14   Baron and Kenny, op. cit.

15   See Clarke, R.V. and Weisburd, D. (1994) Diffusion of Crime Control Benefits: Observations on the Reverse of Displacement, in Clarke, R.V. (ed.), *Crime Prevention Studies*, Vol. 2. Monsey, NY: Criminal Justice Press.

16   Shadish et al., op. cit., p 87.

17   Baron and Kenny, op. cit.

18   Farrington, D.P. and Petrosino, A. (2001) The Campbell Collaboration Crime and Justice Group, *Annals of the American Academy of Political and Social Science*, Vol. 578, pp 35–49.

19   Farrington, D.P., Gottfredson, D.C., Sherman, L.W. and Welsh, B.C. (2002) The Maryland Scientific Methods Scale, in Sherman *et al.*, op. cit., pp 13–21.

20   Cook and Campbell, op. cit.

21   Ibid.

22   Sherman *et al.*, op. cit.

Chapter 7

What Do Offenders Think About CCTV?

Martin Gill and Karryn Loveday[1]

If CCTV has a role to play in crime prevention and detection then there is much to be gained from ascertaining the views of the very people it is targeted at. This paper reports on research findings from face-to-face interviews with offenders in prison, specifically focusing on their opinions of CCTV. Some of the issues addressed include whether CCTV causes them to alter the ways in which they offend; the extent to which they view it as a deterrent; and their views on the types of circumstances and environments in which they perceive CCTV to be a threat. While generally the interviewees did not worry unduly about CCTV in planning their offences, those who had previously been captured by CCTV were more likely to perceive it as a threat than those who had not.

Introduction

Criminologists are gradually beginning to learn more about CCTV, how it works, what its strengths and limitations are and the ways in which it operates with other measures to bring about positive changes in the environment. This learning is still at an early stage, and is reflected in reviews of previous works which have suggested that in terms of its effectiveness the jury on CCTV is still out.[2] One aspect that has been largely ignored up until now has been any detailed consideration of the offenders' perspectives.

There has been very little work on what offenders think about CCTV.[3] This is not especially unusual, as offenders' views are only rarely incorporated into discussions about the effectiveness of different security and crime prevention measures.[4] This surprises some people, including non-criminologists and non-academics who often assume that questioning offenders is the most logical way of gaining insights into whether measures are effective. Given that offending still takes place even when cameras are clearly present, what do offenders think about them and why are these views held? It is principally these questions that this research seeks to answer.

The research is based on interviews with 77 convicted male offenders in prison 19 (24.7 per cent) of these were with young offenders and the remaining 58 (75.3 per cent) with adult offenders. Interviews took place in five prisons (three young offenders and two adult establishments). Prisoners' participation in the study was voluntary, with the only criteria for inclusion being that they had committed (but had not necessarily been caught for or serving a sentence for) a theft[5] or fraud offence in the past.[6] Specifically, 19 discussed street robberies (17 with young offenders, 2 with adult offenders), 25 discussed burglaries (15 young offenders, 10 adults), 26 talked about card frauds (9 young offenders, 17 adult offenders) and 7 were interviewed about shop thefts (5 young offenders, 2 adult offenders). All interviews were conducted on a one-to-one basis where questions focused on offenders' approaches to committing offences and their assessment of the risks involved.[7] This paper reports on their views of CCTV, which were ascertained at various points in the interview.

In each case the offenders were asked whether CCTV had made any difference to their own offending both generally and for the specific offence they discussed. The advantages of discussing these types of offences is that they invite consideration of CCTV in three different environments—in the street, in homes and in businesses. Generally when CCTV is discussed, static systems are considered, but in fact CCTV systems vary quite markedly. Overt redeployable systems which can be moved around to target specific hot spots, offer a different way of combating crime. Offenders were asked whether they thought redeployable CCTV would be a threat to street drug dealers and then were asked about the potential impact of static cameras. At the end of each interview offenders were also invited to respond to some statements about the effectiveness of CCTV. The final part of this paper considers their responses.

Street robbers

The presence of CCTV did not appear to be a major concern for the 19 street robbers. Only 2 reported specifically seeking out a location which did not have CCTV, and while 8 others discussed an offence where CCTV was present, all of them said that CCTV did not affect the way the offence was committed. Six of these admitted wearing a disguise, particularly hooded and reversible clothing; however, they would have worn this anyway to protect their identity. So while they specifically chose locations which reduced the risk, CCTV was not a major element in the assessment of that risk. In short, they worried about being seen, but CCTV cameras were no bigger a threat than anyone or anything else. In fact none of the street robbers were caught by CCTV for the offence which they discussed, although some of those who were interviewed about burglary offences said that CCTV had caught them for robbery offences in the past.

Some noted that the offence was carried out so quickly that the chances of getting caught at the scene were not great and CCTV did not add to the threat:

> 'For me I think it's about speed—do the robbery and then get out of there. Even if you are seen they have to catch you.'

> 'Unless you are unlucky and they have a team [police] working the street, by the time they [the camera] have found you and called for the police you are long gone.'

> 'I'm not wandering around waiting afterwards to get picked up, am I?'

Burglars

Of the 22 burglars interviewed, 12 discussed burglaries on commercial premises and 10 on dwellings. Only 3 (13.6 per cent) committed the burglary they discussed in an area where they believed CCTV was in place, although not all were sure. The 3 burglars who committed their offence in a location covered by CCTV did not consider that it made any difference to the crime—it made it neither harder nor easier. One commented, reflecting the views of street robbers:

> 'It's not like you hang around. You are in and out and away. Just unlucky if they stop you and then they have to find you.'

There appeared to be more pressing concerns than CCTV. For example, 4 commercial burglars commented that they specifically chose to target premises at out-of-town industrial parks on a Saturday night. They believed that the police were likely to be busy in town and would be slow to respond to incidents on the outskirts. This is an important point in terms of policing. Although rural areas seek CCTV cover, offenders appear to believe that the notification of an incident carries no guarantee that the police are able to respond quickly.

More encouragingly, 4 (18.1 per cent) burglars interviewed reported that they had been caught by CCTV when committing offences—2 for robbery, 1 for shoplifting and 1 for burglary. The offender caught by CCTV for the burglary he discussed, claimed he was shocked that the street camera system had focused upon him, even though he knew it was there. He had assumed that it was not monitored but he was later to discover that a 'crack house' in the same street as the house he burgled was being monitored by the police in a special operation. The interviewee had entered the crack house first and was monitored leaving, walking further up the street and entering premises to commit the burglary. He was caught on camera leaving the house in possession of a range of stolen goods, which he loaded into his car. Within the hour he was in police custody.

Despite this experience, this burglar—like the other three caught by CCTV for robbery and shoplifting—did not view CCTV as a major obstacle to overcome when committing burglary:

> 'They should put more [CCTV] where it would make a big difference. Mind you suppose would just go to Manchester and London to rob as my face isn't known on CCTV there.'

> 'Unlucky if they spot you and what they looking for anyway? Even if there are cameras about you're just walking along the street. Go round the back to get in not stand at the front where you can be seen.'

> 'We've got so many cameras man, they can't all be watched. They have to find you, guess what you're going to do and then do something about it.'

Some offered suggestions as to circumstances when CCTV was less effective:

> 'Rain days are good working days cause the cameras can't see as good in the rain.'

> 'If you do a place over at night what difference does CCTV make anyway?'

One burglar believed CCTV had a limited use:

> 'They [the cameras] will be seen and then will be no use—everyone would know it was there. Don't think would make any difference—wasting time when police could be doing other things. CCTV is not all bad, has some good things for kids like making sure they get to school. Should look after kids with CCTV not use it against the public.'

Card fraudsters

There were 26 interviews with offenders who discussed credit card frauds, 16 of which were face-to-face frauds[8] and 10 card-not-present frauds. This section focuses on the perspectives of the 16 face-to-face credit card fraudsters as they had greater exposure to CCTV during the course of their offending.

The real skill of a face-to-face card fraudster is to appear as a 'normal shopper' regardless of what happens during the offence. For example, when a member of staff called the card company during a transaction and said that there was a problem with the card the fraudster actually spoke with the card company and argued with them about the status of the card. He believed that by keeping up the 'front' of being a legitimate shopper he would get away from the shop—and he did. He was able to leave without security or the police being called. Interviewees suggested that it is perhaps because of this core skill of acting as a 'normal shopper' that card fraudsters are not perturbed about CCTV in the stores in which they commit their offences. All 16 face-to-face card fraudsters stated that CCTV made no difference to the way that they committed their offence and they did not consider that it made it more difficult. One fraudster summed up as follows:

> 'What are they looking for? I'm acting the same as everyone else shopping. Why would they look at me? All I do is hand over a card to pay for my goods. I pay—it's not like I've got it stuffed up my shirt trying to get away without paying.'

In any event, some noted reiterating the point made above, they did not advertise their identity and so were not overly worried about the tapes being reviewed afterwards:

> 'All you have to do is keep you head down a bit or wear a cap and they don't get a good look at you—that's if they keep the tape long enough anyway.'

Half of the face-to-face card fraudsters discussed an offence where there was collusion with store staff—they were working in partnership with a member of staff and did not have to consider the risks of being challenged if there was a problem with the status of the credit card for example. This will have contributed to a lack of concern about CCTV or, for that matter, anything else. With complicit staff to assist them these card fraudsters effectively removed all obstacles to the successful commission of the offence. Generally speaking, the biggest danger for this group was the status of the card; there was always the danger that it could have been reported stolen before it was used. While strategies were adopted to minimize the risk, such as purchasing goods over the phone, via the Internet or by attempting to use the card to pay for calls in a telephone kiosk prior to using face-to-face, the time lag in between meant fraudsters could never be sure.

Shop thieves

Seven shop thieves were interviewed (5 young and 2 adult offenders). The adult offenders were more organized than the young offenders for this offence—being 'professional' shoplifters rather than just taking a single item, such as a CD, they would take a large quantity of an item (clothing in all cases) to pass on to a 'fence'.

The shop thieves interviewed did not consider CCTV to be something that made their offence difficult to commit, but it was something they had to consider and 'work around'. Six (85 per cent) felt that it did not make a difference to the offence. However, most of these shop thieves did state that they would 'work' in blind spots and one noted he would turn his back to the camera in an attempt to avoid detection on CCTV. The way in which they stole (blind spots and back to camera) was changed by the presence of CCTV, but this was not thought of as making it 'difficult' for them. The other two shop thieves (both were young offenders) stated that CCTV made it slightly more difficult to steal because it increased their perceptions of the risks of getting caught and the level of nervousness they felt.

CCTV was not felt to be effective in stores that had high displays. This meant that there were 'blind spots', that is areas of the store where they could not easily be seen. Interestingly, 6 (85 per cent) of the 7 shop thieves volunteered that they targeted a particular sports retailer for this reason (and the fact that their goods were highly desirable for passing on for resale[9]). One offender, echoing the position of others, said:

> '[The sports retailer], so easy, no way they can see you with everything [stock] up so high. Great to hide behind and help yourself.'

The shop thieves were not aware when and whether the CCTV system was being monitored and only 2 (28.5 per cent) had been caught by CCTV (both young offenders).

CCTV and street drug crime

The 77 offenders were asked whether they felt that the use of CCTV (type not specified) would make it more difficult for people to deal in drugs on the street. The principle of redeployable CCTV was then explained and a similar question asked—would redeployable CCTV make it more difficult for a street drug dealer to operate and avoid detection. The questions enabled the different types of CCTV systems to be compared.

Only 5 (6.5 per cent) interviewees thought that static CCTV made it more difficult to deal in drugs on the street.

The idea of redeployable CCTV was new to most interviewees but they did not view it as a threat or a very imaginative idea. However, 7 (9.1 per cent) felt using redeployable CCTV would make it harder for street drug dealers. This does not mean, however, that they considered it would necessarily yield positive results in the battle against street drug dealing—merely make the dealers have to work harder:

'It makes it harder 'coz you have to move somewhere else but it won't stop you.'

'So you have to work smarter—that's not such a bad thing, is it?'

Therefore, while the concept of redeployable CCTV caused only 2 (2.6 per cent) offenders to change their opinion from the one they held when static CCTV was discussed, the rest remained sceptical:

'How much do they get paid for thinking this stuff up? Not as much as I do for dealing, but I won't mind their job if that's what they have to do.'

'Here, I don't have a degree but I've got a Merc. Dealing bought me that car and they think I'm a muppet who will fall for this shit?'

'They are as stupid as they think we are.'

Some made the point that drug dealing was a business activity and the threat would have to be much greater if it was to seriously challenge the activity:

'It's not like on the telly you know—dealers run a business and are smart enough to get around that shit.'

'Those cameras would not last five minutes—this is business and money and they make too much to let them [the cameras] get in the way.'

'It's about money and so them cameras wouldn't stand a chance.'

There was no significant difference in the opinions held between those who had experience of the street drug scene and those who did not.

When interviewees were asked about the value of static CCTV in combating street drug dealing, 82.7 per cent (62) of the sample did not think it would be effective. Of these, 71 per cent (44) had street drug experience and 29 per cent (18) had not. When asked about the perceived impact of redeployable CCTV, 77.9 per cent (60) did not think it would be effective, 69.4 per cent (41) of whom had street drug scene experience and 31.6 per cent (19) did not.

Once again similar points were made in that it was not felt that street drug dealers would necessarily need to change the way in which they operated to combat the use of CCTV:

'Look, it's not like you are standing there in the open making the deals. The way you work no one looking would see any gear passing hands anyway.'

'It's not like you stand there obvious, most people wouldn't even know dealing was going on. There's nothing to see so how would the camera get anything?'

'Lady, you think they stand there like they is selling moody [counterfeit] perfume?'

'They [cameras] can't see everywhere—they all have blind spots. All you got to do is work out your angles and you're safe.'

'If I can dip a wallet I can palm some gear over just as quick and just as nimble. You won't even have realized that I'd just done business.'

'At the end of the day you will have to work a bit harder but pick your blind spot and set up stall.'

Those who had not been captured by CCTV (54, 85.7 per cent) were more likely than those who had been captured (9, 64.3 per cent) to argue that static cameras would not impact upon the street drug scene.[10]

CCTV in perspective

At the end of the interview offenders were asked a number of fixed alternative answer questions about CCTV and the answers are displayed in Tables 1–3 below. It needs to be stressed that in this question they were not being asked about their offences specifically, but rather about their general views, albeit that they were based on personal experiences. And it should be stressed that most interviewees had committed a range of offences, not just the type that were interviewed about and reported above. Table 1 reports on questions directed at whether CCTV made stealing more difficult and increased the chances of getting caught.[11]

Table 1. Whether CCTV increased the risk involved in offending

All offenders (74)	Strongly agree	Agree	Neutral	Disagree	Strongly disagree
CCTV in store makes it more difficult to steal	—	18 (24.3%)	6 (8.1%)	46 (63.8%)	4 (5.4%)
CCTV increases the chances of getting caught	—	34 (45.9%)	5 (6.7%)	34 (45.9%)	1 (1.3%)
Town-centre CCTV is a real impediment to coming into the area to steal	3 (4%)	21 (28.3%)	12 (16.2%)	36 (48.6%)	2 (2.7%)

No one strongly agreed with the statements that CCTV made theft difficult or increased the chances of getting caught, and less than a quarter in the first case and much less than a half in the second case agreed at all. Almost a third of interviewees agreed that town-centre CCTV was an impediment, but more than half did not think so. However, a principal difference emerged between those who had been captured because of CCTV pictures in the past and those alternatively described as not captured.[12] In all, 14 (18.1 per cent) of the sample stated that they had been captured. While the majority (9, 64.3 per cent) of this group agreed that the presence of CCTV in a store makes it more difficult to steal, only a minority (15, 23.8 per cent) of the non-captured agreed.[13] Similarly, the captured were more likely to agree that CCTV increased the chances of being caught (10, 71.4 per cent) than the non-captured (41.3 per cent, 26).[14] The comparative figures for views on whether town-centre CCTV was an impediment to offenders going into that area to steal were less disparate, in this case 6 (42.9 per cent) against 36 (57.1 per cent)—and were not significant.

Most interviewees noted that the mere existence of cameras did not change the situation dramatically, although the fact that there were pictures meant that the police were more likely to be called. This point was confirmed in their responses to the statement displayed in Table 2.

Table 2. Whether CCTV encourages police attendance

All offenders (74)	Strongly agree	Agree	Neutral	Disagree	Strongly disagree
Police more likely to be called if store has CCTV evidence	1 (1.3%)	53 (71.6%)	6 (8.1%)	14 (18.9%)	— —

Once again, the 'captured' were more likely than the 'not captured' to believe that CCTV evidence was more likely to result in the police being called.[15]

Most held the belief that pictures contained an additional danger, although not all felt that this itself meant imminent danger; any danger would depend on the quality of the images. Some interviewees showed the researcher copies of CCTV images that were alleged to be of them. None of these images were clear and an accurate identification appeared difficult. The poor image quality was viewed as an opportunity to plead not guilty, as they could not accurately be identified. However, this was not a view that they all held, as Table 3 shows.

Table 3. Offenders' views on picture quality

All offenders (74)	Strongly agree	Agree	Neutral	Disagree	Strongly disagree
CCTV picture quality is generally poor	2 (2.7%)	17 (22.9%)	25 (33.7%)	27 (36.4%)	3 (4%)

More than 4 in 10 disagreed that picture quality was poor, while 3 in 10 were 'neutral', perhaps because image quality varied and was sometimes poor and sometimes very good. Over a fifth believed that the picture quality was generally poor.[16] The captured, arguably possessing more direct experience of CCTV, were more likely than the not captured to believe that picture quality was generally poor. Clearly there is an opportunity for crime prevention here. Should the images become clearer and there is a chance to back it up with other evidence, then the opportunities would be greater to impress upon offenders the heightened risks of being apprehended.

Discussion

Interviewees generally held negative opinions of CCTV. Although 32 (41.5 per cent) of our offenders discussed an offence which took place where CCTV was installed, only two of these (2.59 per cent of the total sample) felt that it made their offence more difficult to commit—both were young offenders who shoplifted. It was clear during interviews that the initial response to CCTV was negative—that it would not catch them and, if it did, they were just unlucky. However, when the issue was discussed further it became apparent that they did attach some element of risk to CCTV, given that they chose to wear particular clothing or work blind spots.

While most thought that CCTV (either in stores or in town centres) does not make it more difficult to steal, it clearly poses different dangers. The same proportion of offenders felt that it increased the chances of getting caught as those who did not, and the majority were of the view that CCTV increased the chances of the police being involved. However, there was scepticism about picture quality.

Overall, the evidence suggests that most offenders do not appear to see CCTV as a threat in the individual crimes they commit. Offenders felt that they could conceal their identity by wearing a disguise and/or by looking away from the camera, and most were of the view that the picture quality was poor. Moreover, many did not feel that they, and others who commit crimes in view, were sufficiently blatant enough for cameras to easily spot what is going on and offences take place quickly. Although pictures may be used later to identify and support a prosecution this was not seen as a major worry—some noting that the police lacked resources to follow-up on potential evidence—and certainly much less of a priority than the immediate need for money to fund drug habits.

However, this somewhat negative view needs to be balanced. Often offenders would not know that CCTV had helped identify them, especially if images were not part of the prosecution case. In practice CCTV may have played a role in raising initial suspicion about their activities, in helping to identify them or (and this has rarely been mentioned in the context of CCTV) in helping to provide forensic evidence against them. For example, CCTV images could show a suspect discarding a cigarette near the scene which, if retrieved, could show they were there. CCTV could show them leaning against a window enabling a print to be obtained, thus showing they were at the location and helping the police to use the evidence as part of building up a case.

There is potentially a lot more CCTV can offer to crime detection, not least where offenders underestimate the effectiveness of it. Of course some offenders are caught on camera and those who had been caught previously held different views and were significantly more likely to see it as a threat. For advocates of CCTV there is evidence for optimism in this finding. Thus as picture quality gets better, as operators become better trained and as the police learn to use the technology to greatest advantage, so the benefits of CCTV can be used to catch offenders. Nevertheless, it is likely that for CCTV to be truly effective it will need to be introduced alongside other measures.

In short, CCTV was not perceived to be a threat by the offenders interviewed. Any potential threat from CCTV was lessened by the speed and manner in which the offence was committed. For example, street robbery and street drug dealing are, typically, both swift offences. Offenders also felt that the any potential threat from being observed on camera was reduced by the lack of police back-up on the ground and many doubted that the cameras were properly monitored. Confidence in the operator's ability to 'snap' a good quality image of an offender was low among the sample. However, offenders were not left completely unperturbed by the presence of CCTV and risks were mitigated by disguising themselves (hats and hooded reversible clothing) as well as turning away from the direct view of the camera and working in blind spots. However, those who had previously been captured by CCTV were more likely to perceive it as a threat than those who had not.

Notes

1   Professor Martin Gill is Director of Perpetuity Research and Consultancy International (PRCI) Ltd and a Professor of Criminology at the University of Leicester; email: m.gill@perpetuitygroup.com. Karryn Loveday is the Crime and Disorder Officer for the Safer Middlesborough Partnership; email: karryn_loveday@middlesborough.gov.uk. The authors would like to thank Kate Collins, Ross Little and Dave Mackay for their comments on an earlier draft of the paper.

2   See Walsh, B. and Farrington, D. (2002) *Crime Prevention Effects of Close Circuit Television: A Systematic Review*. London: Home Office.

3   There has been a study of those arrested on suspicion of having committed a crime who often viewed CCTV as being useful for protecting their rights; see Newburn, T. and Hayman, S. (2002) *Policing, Surveillance, and Social Control: CCTV and Police Monitoring of Suspects*. Cullompton: Willan.

4   For a summary of offenders' views on security, see Gill, M. (2000) *Commercial Robbery*. Oxford: Blackstone Press.

5   For the purposes of this study 'theft' offences were primarily street robbery, burglary and shoplifting and 'fraud' offences were primarily credit card fraud.

6   For validity purposes, where the respondent reported that they had been convicted for the offence they were interviewed about, their prison records were checked for confirmation. In all cases the data were valid.

7   Given the way the sample was generated there is no claim of representativeness here and caution is advised in extrapolating these findings. Thus the views, at best, help to generate insights into issues which need to be assessed alongside data generated from other sources.

8   Typically face-to-face card fraud takes the form of the fraudster presenting the card as a means of payment to, for example, a cashier. This differs from card-not-present fraud which is typically, although not exclusively, carried out over the telephone or Internet where only the card number rather than the card itself is provided. In these circumstances there is no direct personal contact with another individual.

9   This same sports retailer was also mentioned by many of the credit card fraudsters due to the collusion of staff or their apparent lack of knowledge in terms of card fraud, coupled with the desirability and ease of resale of their goods.

10   Fischer's Test $p < 0.01$.

11   All tables are based on 74 responses—3 of the sample declined to answer this section of the interview.

12   Other variables, including age, self-reported success rate and type of offence did not explain any differences in findings in the data.

13   Fischer's Test $p < 0.01$.

14    $\times 2 = 5.9 \ p < 0.05$,

15   This was not quite statistically significant.

16   Fischer's Test $p < 0.001$.

Chapter 8

Does CCTV Displace Crime? An Evaluation of the Evidence and a Case Study from Amsterdam

Sander Flight, Yvonne van Heerwaarden, Paul van Soomeren[1]

Most studies that have tried to assess the amount of displacement caused by CCTV have found that displacement can occur, but that only rarely can complete displacement be observed. The net result has therefore always been positive. An evaluation of three CCTV schemes in Amsterdam confirms these findings.

These schemes showed positive results in the CCTV areas themselves. Police and survey data in and around the areas show that crime decreased, and a slight but significant reduction in fear of crime could be observed in one of the three areas. There were no signs that fear of crime had been displaced to—had become higher in—adjacent areas. A slight decrease in crime in the streets surrounding the CCTV project could be observed. However, there are differences in the degree of displacement of different types of crimes. Assaults, muggings, and thefts from cars increased significantly in the so-called 'probable displacement area'.

Introduction

The first projects using security cameras—or closed circuit television (CCTV)—in public spaces in the Netherlands date back to 1997. Only six years later in January 2003 more than 80 of the country's 550 municipalities were using CCTV in public places—in entertainment districts, shopping centres, car parks, industrial areas and public transport. CCTV has become a hot issue in the Netherlands. In recent years, more and more Dutch research has been published on the effects of CCTV. Although it is at the forefront of political and public debate on CCTV, one possible effect of CCTV has received relatively little attention in that research: displacement of crime. This paper will focus on displacement by presenting the empirical results of a CCTV evaluation in the city of Amsterdam. But first, this paper looks into some theoretical issues regarding displacement and international research on displacement and CCTV.

Displacement theory

Displacement means that criminal behaviour is continued at a different location or in a different way as a result of preventive measures. In the literature a distinction is made between five types of displacement:[2]

- *geographical displacement*—the same offence is committed in a different area;

- *temporal displacement*—offenders commit the same offence, but at a different time, for example during the period when the camera is not running;

- *tactical displacement*—the way in which the offence is committed (the modus operandi) changes. For example, offenders make sure that they cannot be identified;

- *target displacement*—criminal behaviour takes on a different target;

- *crime type displacement*—in this type of displacement, an offender switches from one type of crime to another which is less easy to recognize on camera.

Combinations of the various types of displacement are also possible.

Research on displacement has consistently shown that the net result of preventive measures is almost always positive: the problem may have been displaced to a certain extent, but this displacement is almost never complete. In the following section, empirical results from several studies looking into displacement caused by CCTV are presented.

The degree to which displacement occurs could well be influenced to a considerable degree by the perceptions of (potential) offenders.[3] If they perceive preventive measures to be limited to a specific area (or specific time, specific object, etc.) there is a high probability of displacement. When, on the other hand, offenders feel that this specific measure is just one of many ways in which the government is clamping down on crime in general, a specific preventive measure like CCTV can contribute to an improvement beyond the area at which the measure was originally targeted. Hence the perceived scope of a preventive measure may be bigger than its objective scope. Some research even shows that preventive measures in one area can have a positive knock-on effect: not only did the situation in the target area improve, but positive effects were also measured in areas outside the target area itself.[4]

Displacement probably depends to a considerable degree on the type of offender involved. One useful division in types of offenders is that between generalists and specialists. Generalists are flexible in their criminal behaviour and will find alternative ways to commit offences when confronted with preventive measures. For example, if there are cameras inside shops, these offenders could switch to street-mugging or car crime. Displacement is therefore likely if the offenders active in an area are generalists. Specialists, on the other hand, are not as flexible because they have a specific skill (e.g. burglary of a certain type of residence, or theft of or from a certain brand of car). Their ability to displace their criminal activities is limited. It may therefore be expected that the introduction of CCTV in a certain area, specifically targeted at protecting the objects they favour, will not lead to displacement but to a decrease of the number of offences they commit. There is no reason to assume a priori that the theoretical approach to the problem of displacement in general does not apply to CCTV.

Displacement—international empirical findings

Almost all international research on crime displacement shows that the net result of the preventive measures taken is positive. Sometimes there is displacement, but it is never complete. The first systematic research on crime displacement was conduced in the 1990s. The first studies from Canada[5] and the United States[6] showed that displacement was a much smaller problem than was generally assumed. The most authoritative international study came from the Netherlands.[7] A total of 55 projects from eight countries, including Great Britain, the United States and the Netherlands, were studied. In 16 studies, no displacement effect was observed and in 33 studies, partial displacement was observed. In six studies, the preventive measures had an effect not only in the project area but also beyond—a positive knock-on effect. The study concluded that displacement is a possibility, but that it is certainly not a natural consequence of crime prevention or crime reduction schemes. Even if displacement occurs, it is never complete. A striking result was that this appeared to be true for all offences, striking because it was generally assumed that certain offences, for instance drug dealing, are almost completely autonomous and not to be influenced by preventive measures. Addicts and drug dealers depend on this type of crime and will therefore find another place, time or way to close the deal. This assumption proved to be untrue; Cromwell[8] showed that addicts take into account the consequences of their actions and are in fact influenced by preventive measures. Other research showed similar findings.[9]

Research into crime displacement as a result of CCTV is still quite rare, although some research into CCTV does pay explicit attention to displacement:

- In Birmingham, it appeared that CCTV did not lead to geographical displacement, but that it did lead to functional—or crime type—displacement: mugging and pickpocketing decreased, whereas theft from cars increased.[10]

- In Newcastle, no geographical or functional displacement effects were observed. Here, there was even a positive knock-on effect outside the camera area and in particular with respect to vandalism and burglaries.[11]

- In Airdrie, indications were found that CCTV led to positive effects in the camera area *and* outside the area.[12]

- In the centre of Copenhagen, CCTV led to a decrease of mugging in the group of offenders who were not dependent on the money. Among those who were dependent on the money, mugging increased.[13]

- In Doncaster, no displacement was observed. According to the author, the observed increase in the control area is a consequence of 'pre-existing trends'.[14]

- In Ilford it was shown that mugging and burglary was displaced from the city centre (where the cameras were located) to the surrounding neighbourhoods.[15]

- In Burnley, CCTV had a positive knock-on effect for violent crime and car crime. Burglary did seem to have been displaced.[16]

- In Cincinnati, no displacement was found in one of the two projects studied; it was found in the other. In that project there seemed to be a shift in the offenders' activities, 'given the increase in the number of civilian phone calls to the police'.[17]

- In Cambridge, where 30 cameras were installed in the centre, crime proved to have dropped, but less than in the surrounding area. The researchers qualified this as an undesired effect of CCTV; the number of reports to the police and crimes logged by the police increased, while surveys showed that the number of offences had not decreased.[18]

Summarizing these results, partial displacement was observed in two cases. In the other cases either there was no displacement at all (two projects), there was a positive knock-on effect outside the camera area as well (two projects), or the results were not clear. All in all, the balance in displacement research specifically focusing on CCTV seems to tend towards positive net results, thereby confirming the general theory on displacement. The question whether this conclusion also applies to the CCTV projects in Amsterdam is the central issue in the next section of this paper.

Three CCTV schemes in Amsterdam

In Amsterdam, three experiments with CCTV in public areas are being conducted.[19] One experiment started as early as 1997 (Kraaiennest), one in September 2000 (August Allebéplein) and one in mid-2001 (Belgiëplein) (see Figure 1). All three areas are medium-sized shopping areas surrounded by houses and apartment buildings. The character of the three areas differs considerably. The Kraaiennest scheme is located in a part of Amsterdam generally regarded as a problematic area. The other two areas are less problematic, although here too the level of crime and incivilities is relatively high compared to the average situation in the city.

Figure 1. Map of Amsterdam with the three CCTV locations

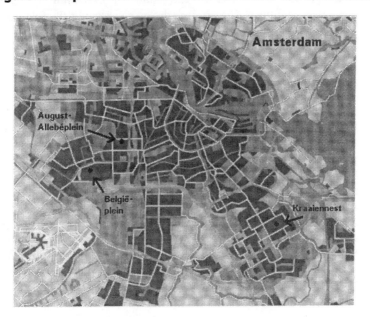

The CCTV scheme in Kraaiennest is not only older than the other two but also larger: here, 20 cameras are operational, the images are recorded permanently and preserved for seven days in order to enable police investigations after crimes have been committed. The monitors are watched live by operators from Monday till Saturday from 8 am until 10.30 pm. The two other schemes in the western part of Amsterdam are smaller: four (August Allebéplein) and five cameras (Belgiëplein) are operational there. An operator is only present during so-called 'peak hours': Thursday, Friday and Saturday from 3 pm until 11 pm. Images are never recorded here unless an operator is present and he or she decides it is useful to record them.

The aims of the three CCTV schemes differ: in the two projects in the West of Amsterdam (August Allebéplein and Belgiëplein), the aim was mainly to do something about loitering youth and, to a lesser degree, end street fights and robberies. The business community in these areas gave a powerful impulse to the introduction of CCTV. The other scheme (Kraaiennest) was mostly targeted at trouble caused by drug trading and drug use. Also, there was a large number of muggings. In an attempt to turn the tables, CCTV was chosen as one of a larger number of preventive measures to be introduced.

Research design

In the beginning of 2001, the city of Amsterdam asked the private research and consultancy bureau DSP-groep to carry out an evaluation of the three experiments then running.[20] The research design consisted of the following four steps:

1. A literature study of national and international research on the effects of CCTV with special focus on displacement effects.

2. An analysis of police records for the year before and the year following the introduction of CCTV in the three different areas. Also, in order to be able to control for large-scale trends in recorded crime, police records were analyzed for wider areas encompassing the CCTV areas: the police team area (approximately 5,000 inhabitants), the police district (of which there are eight in the city of Amsterdam) and the police region of Amsterdam (with around three-quarters of a million inhabitants). Because the cameras were not installed at the same time, the time periods analyzed differ by location. In Kraaiennest and August Allebéplein the research was divided into a 12-month period before and a 12-month period after September 2000. At Belgiëplein, the start of the project was later, therefore the two periods analyzed here were the year preceding and the year following March 2001.

3. A survey conducted in two sweeps one year apart—June 2001 and June 2002.[21] Three groups of users of the areas were interviewed: shopkeepers in the squares (the same people were interviewed in the first and second sweep), inhabitants (minimum of 100 at each location) and visitors (minimum of 100 at each location). Overall, 2,000 questionnaires were completed.[22]

4. In-depth interviews with police officers, camera operators, policy-makers and others involved in the organization and deployment of CCTV in the three areas. This part of the research was mostly used to put the other findings into perspective.

The most important research questions to be answered were:

- Does CCTV reduce crime and incivilities (e.g. loitering youth, verbal aggression,[23] etc.)?
- Does CCTV make people feel safer?
- Does CCTV displace crime and incivilities?
- Does CCTV lead to a shift in fear of crime or feelings of insecurity from the CCTV areas to other (adjacent) areas?

Because of the attention given to the problem of displacement, it was decided to invest a considerable part of the research budget in this subject. One area was chosen where there were no cameras, but which was likely to become a displacement area. For this, the streets surrounding one of the CCTV areas, the August Allebéplein, were chosen. This choice was made because of the high displacement risk in this specific area. The streets around August Allebéplein share some important characteristics with the square itself: there are shops in both locations and the areas are similar in many other respects. The selected 'probable displacement area' is next to August Allebéplein: it was envisaged that offenders would shift their activities 'round the corner' without too much trouble. In fact, immediately after installation of the cameras on the square, there was the feeling among some residents, politicians and police officers that car thefts were displaced from the square itself to the other side of an apartment building located on one side of the square. Therefore, if displacement did occur, it would probably occur here, making it an ideal area to test the displacement hypothesis. To do this, exactly the same research activities were undertaken in the streets surrounding August Allebéplein: two sweeps of surveys among inhabitants, visitors and local shopkeepers, an analysis of police records and in-depth interviews with local officials and police officers.[24]

Of course, it would have been even better if this 'extra' research could also have been carried out in the two other areas, but there was no budget for that option. However, police records were also analyzed for the surroundings of the other two CCTV areas. Also, some extra questions were asked in the surveys among residents and visitors to assess the amount of displacement experienced or observed by them. So, albeit indirectly, for these two other areas an indication of the amount of displacement can also be given.

Reduction of crime and incivilities

Though the rest of this paper will mainly focus on displacement, a summary of the general effect of the schemes may be of some interest too.

Police data
Though not very reliable due to the fact that a lot of crime goes unrecorded, the police figures for five types of crime (street robbery, assault, hold-up, burglary and car crime) show a decrease in the three CCTV areas taken together from 436 a year to 362 a year (a drop of 74), while the figures for the surrounding police team area, police district and the whole Amsterdam police region show a rising or more or less constant trend.[25]

Survey data
The surveys among residents of the CCTV areas show a marked decrease in incidents of 23 per cent as shown in Table 1.

Table 1. Type of crime and incivilities: victim percentage among residents in all three CCTV areas

	2001 %	2002 %	Change
Mugging	5	7	+2
Burglary	4	6	+2
Pickpocketing	5	4	−1
Theft from car	16	15	−1
Assault	8	6	−2
Bicycle theft	8	5	−3*
Trouble caused by groups of youngsters	28	23	−5
Verbal aggression	25	18	−7**
Other offences/incivilities	11	4	−7***
Total number of crimes/incivilities (absolute)	**438**	**362**	**−23**
Number of respondents (absolute)	**397**	**413**	

Significance level: *p<0.10; **p<0.05; ***p<0.01.

Reduction of fear of crime

The vast majority of residents do occasionally feel unsafe in all three areas investigated. This was shown in the 2001 survey as well as in the 2002 survey. The proportion of residents indicating they felt unsafe once in a while in 'their' CCTV area was roughly three in four (Belgiëplein and Kraaiennest), but rose to 91 per cent (August Allebéplein, 2001 sweep). No significant improvement between the 2001 and 2002 surveys was found, except on August Allebéplein, where the percentage of residents feeling unsafe decreased from 91 to 82 per cent during the year. So, as far as feelings of insecurity are concerned, a slight improvement could be observed in only one of the three CCTV areas.

Displacement of fear of crime

The Amsterdam research on CCTV focused strongly on the displacement of crime and incivilities, as well as fear of crime. This was largely due to the fact that local authorities and policy-makers think or say that cameras 'won't help a bit because crime will simply be displaced round the corner'. To test this displacement hypothesis, extra research was done in one of the three CCTV areas: August Allebéplein in the western part of Amsterdam. Next to this square a 'probable displacement area' was identified, which had very similar characteristics to the square itself: two streets with residential buildings with shops facing the street.

Table 2. Fear of crime—change in the percentage of residents that is sometimes afraid of crime on the street in the CCTV area and in the streets around that area

	CCTV area			Surrounding area		
	2001 %	2002 %	Change	2001 %	2002 %	Change
August Allebéplein	91	82	−9**	81	80	−1
Belgiëplein	77	76	−1	63	64	+1
Kraaiennest	78	82	+4	89	85	−4

Significance level: **$p < 0.05$.
Source: Survey in two sweeps among residents of the three CCTV areas and the 'probable displacement area' area surrounding August Allebéplein. See note 22 for the number of respondents in each sweep and at each location. At August Allebéplein, surveys were conducted among residents of the CCTV area itself and a separate survey was conducted among residents of the streets around the square (the so-called 'probable displacement area') so in this case the figures result from direct measurement. The question that was put to both groups was how safe they feel in their own street. At Belgiëplein and Kraaiennest there was only one survey; here the question was asked how safe one felt in the CCTV area as well as in the surrounding area (indirect measurement).

Table 2 shows the results for August Allebéplein (the CCTV area) and the surrounding streets (the 'probable displacement area'). Though no extra displacement area surveys could be held next to the other two CCTV areas (Belgiëplein and Kraaiennest) a rough indication of displacement was available since these residents were not only asked how safe they felt in their own (CCTV) area, but also how safe they felt in the streets surrounding 'their' CCTV area.

So for Belgiëplein and Kraaiennest, the scores presented in Table 2 could be called 'indirect' measures as opposed to the 'direct' measures that are available for August Allebéplein and its neighbourhood.

As mentioned before, a significant improvement in the levels of fear was found in the CCTV area of August Allebéplein where the percentage of residents feeling unsafe decreased from 91 to 82 per cent (see Table 2: −9 per cent). This improvement has not led to an increase of feelings of insecurity in the area surrounding August Allebéplein (the 'probable displacement area'). Here, the surveys show nearly no change: the percentage of residents feeling unsafe decreased from 81 to 80 per cent (−1 per cent). In the other two areas the effects are very limited in the CCTV areas as well as in the surrounding areas. All in all there are no signs that feelings of insecurity have been displaced.

Displacement of crime and incivilities

At August Allebéplein, the surveys among inhabitants showed that the number of crimes and incivilities in the CCTV area itself had fallen substantially between the 2001 and 2002 surveys. The total number of crimes and incivilities dropped from 230 incidents in the 2001 survey to 154 incidents the following year. In the 'probable displacement area' around the CCTV area the number of crimes and incivilities also dropped but by far less: from 103 in 2001 to 97 in 2002. Table 3 shows the results in more detail.

Table 3 shows that the improvement is not equally distributed over all offences. Statistically significant results are found for verbal aggression (−12 per cent), bicycle theft (−8 per cent) and the group of 'other offences' (−10 per cent). In the displacement area, the total number of crimes and incivilities also fell, albeit less spectacularly, by 6 per cent. However, three types of crime seem to have increased here: mugging (+8 per cent), theft from cars (+7 per cent) and assault (+6 per cent). In the CCTV area itself, these crimes did not show a significant change; they either fell (theft from cars and assault) or stayed nearly constant (mugging). This suggests that these three types of crime might have been displaced.

For other types of crime and incivilities, positive effects can be signalled in the displacement area. A statistically significant improvement was found for 'other crimes' (−9 per cent). Two types of crime suggest a positive development (verbal aggression and trouble caused by groups of youngsters; both −9 per cent). Looking at these three crimes and incivilities, a decrease (sometimes statistically significant, sometimes not) can be observed in the CCTV area, indicating a positive knock-on effect.

Table 3. Difference in victim rates for nine crimes between first sweep and second sweep at August Allebéplein versus the 'probable displacement area' (the streets immediately next to the square)

	August Allebéplein ('CCTV area')			Streets around August Allebéplein ('displacement area')		
	2001 %	2002 %	Change	2001 %	2002 %	Change
Verbal aggression	46	34	−12*	23	15	−9
Trouble by groups of youngsters	45	36	−9	28	19	−9
Bicycle theft	15	7	−8**	11	8	−4
Theft from cars	35	27	−7	6	13	+7*
Assault	9	4	−4	4	10	+6*
Pickpocketing	3	3	0	4	7	+3
Mugging	6	7	+1	6	14	+8**
Burglary	5	8	+3	9	10	+1
Other offences	18	8	−10**	11	3	−9**
Number of respondents (absolute)	126	113		98	117	

Significance level: *p < 0.10; **p < 0.05.
Source: Survey among residents 2001 and 2002.
Rounding of the numbers to whole figures (without decimal), causes the difference of one per cent in a few instances.

Experts on CCTV

The possibility of displacement was also a topic in the in-depth interviews held with experts in the CCTV areas: police officers, city council officials, the business community, etc. Some of them were of the opinion that there was displacement, albeit partial, of crime and incivilities. They pointed mostly to loitering youth: after the introduction of CCTV these youngsters reportedly moved from the CCTV area in the middle of the square to the edges, into the doorways of houses and flats. This, in turn, has led to more minor confrontations between residents and youngsters. This has had a positive effect on their behaviour. When asked about more serious crimes such as car crime, muggings and bicycle theft, most experts seem to agree that there has been a partial displacement as well. However, these impressions were not supported by police and survey data.

One effect of CCTV has been the demand for more CCTV in other squares and streets. Officials hesitate to take this road, because there may be other, less expensive, measures to tackle specific crime problems. Increasing CCTV schemes in problem areas could set in motion an almost insatiable appetite for ever more cameras among inhabitants of problem areas, shopkeepers and the public in general.

Conclusion

Most studies that have tried to assess the amount of displacement caused by CCTV have found that displacement can occur, but that only seldom can complete displacement be observed. The net result has therefore always been positive. Our research in Amsterdam confirms these findings: some crimes may have been displaced, but the net result was positive: the total number of crimes committed in the CCTV area fell, and there was also a slight decrease in the streets surrounding the CCTV project. However, a clear difference between different types of crimes was shown. Assaults, muggings and thefts from cars increased significantly in the so-called 'probable displacement area'. On the other hand, there are some types of crimes or incivilities where a positive knock-on effect was indicated. Statistically speaking, this can only be concluded for the category 'other offences', but with a little less statistical rigour, the same pattern is visible for trouble caused by groups of youngsters, verbal aggression and bicycle theft. The percentage of victims of these types of crime decreased in the CCTV area itself, but also in the surrounding streets. But again, these last three findings are not statistically significant, so it is risky to draw firm conclusions. In that respect the same goes for the police figures presented in this paper.

Next to the number of crimes, attention was also paid to fear of crime or feelings of insecurity. It appears that CCTV had little effect on this subjective side of safety, although there was one exception: August Allebéplein. Here, a decrease in the number of people feeling unsafe could be observed. In the area surrounding the CCTV area (the 'probable displacement area') no increase was observed, indicating that there was no displacement.

It is not the first time that displacement research shows that displacement is a potential, but not unavoidable, effect of preventive action and crime reduction schemes. In none of the studies mentioned in this paper was complete displacement observed. On the contrary: in a considerable number of cases there seemed to be a positive knock-on effect beyond the actual area where CCTV is operational.

All in all, it seems justified to conclude that CCTV does not always lead to displacement of crime and incivilities. Based on a theoretical view of offenders, we believe that the key to a successful CCTV project lies in changing the perceptions of offenders. When they become convinced that their criminal or troublemaking behaviour is no longer tolerated—either in the CCTV area or elsewhere—it is most likely that they will adjust their behaviour. If we are correct in assuming that the success of CCTV depends to a considerable degree on the perceived scope of the measure, it would be advisable to invest more in this perceptive aspect of CCTV projects. For instance, pessimistic or fatalistic remarks from police and/or policy-makers implementing another CCTV project ('We're doing the best we can but the offenders will probably just move to the next street') do not contribute to a change in mentality among offenders. In order for preventive measures such as CCTV to be effective in tackling crime and incivilities, it is important that actions are part of a coordinated approach to changing attitudes towards crime. The actual installation of cameras is just one part of this procedure. After all, a camera itself is not much more than a box of electronics with a lens and a wire attached to it. Only when all stakeholders involved (local council, public prosecutor, police, shop owners/keepers, housing associations, private security guards, etc.) work together in a well orchestrated partnership, and CCTV is thus part of a package of measures, can positive effects be achieved, both within and outside the camera area.

Notes

1   Sander Flight is a senior researcher in the field of crime prevention at DSP-groep in Amsterdam; email sflight@zonnet.nl. Yvonne van Heerwaarden also works for DSP-groep in the field of crime prevention. Paul van Soomeren is one of the founders and directors of the board of DSP-groep. DSP-groep (founded in 1984 and formerly known as 'Van Dijk Van Soomeren and Partners') is a privately owned company active in research, consultancy and project/interim management in various fields of expertise such as crime, sports, youth, education, social policy, urban planning, minorities, etc. DSP-groep specializes in quantitative and qualitative research and employs 60 people. DSP-groep works for local, regional, national and European authorities and institutes as well as the private sector. See *http://www.dsp-groep.nl.*

2   Felson, M. and Clarke, R.V. (1998) *Opportunity Makes the Thief: Practical Theory for Crime Prevention*, Police Research Series Paper 98. London: Home Office Research, Development and Statistics Directorate.

3   Clarke R.V. (ed.) (1992) *Situational Crime Prevention: Successful Case Studies.* New York: Harrow & Heston.

4   Bennet, T. and Wright, R. (1984) *Burglars on Burglary*. Aldershot: Gower, and Hesseling, R.B.P. (1994) *Stoppen of verplaatsen? Een literatuuronderzoek over gelegenheidsbeperkende preventie en displacement van criminaliteit*. Arnhem: Gouda Quint (Onderzoek en beleid/WODC).

5   Gabor, T. (1990) Crime Displacement and Situational Prevention: Towards the Development of some Principles, *Canadian Journal of Criminology*, Vol. 32, pp 41–74.

6   Eck, J. E. (1993) The Threat of Crime Displacement, *Criminal Justice Abstract*, Vol. 25, pp 527–546.

7   Hesseling, op. cit.

8   Cromwell *et al.* (1991) *Breaking and Entering: An Ethnographic Analysis of Burglary*. Newbury Park, CA: Sage.

9   Chenery, S., Holt, J. and Pease, K. (1997) *Biting Back II: Reducing Repeat Victimisation in Huddersfield*, Crime Detection and Prevention Paper 82. London: Home Office, and: Brown, B. (1995) *CCTV in Town Centres: Three Case Studies*, Crime Detection and Prevention Series Paper 68. London: Home Office.

10   Brown, B., op. cit.

11   Ibid.

12   Short, E. and Ditton, J. (1995) *Does CCTV Prevent Crime? An Evaluation of the Use of CCTV Surveillance Cameras in Airdrie Town Centre*. Edinburgh: Scottish Office.

13   Carstensen, N. and Birkholm Frederiksen, K. (1997) Situational Crime Prevention, in Ravn L. (ed.), *Kriminalistisk Arbog*. Copenhagen: Criminal Procedure Institute.

14   Skinns, D. (1998) Crime Reduction, Diffusion and Displacement: Evaluating the Effectiveness of CCTV, in Norris, C., Moran, J. and Armstrong, G. (eds), *Surveillance, CCTV and Social Control*. Aldershot: Ashgate.

15   Squires, P. (1998) *An Evaluation of the Ilford Town Centre CCTV Scheme*. Brighton: University of Brighton.

16   Armitage, R., Smyth, G. and Pease. K. (1999) Burnley CCTV evaluation, in Painter, K. and Tilley, N. (eds), *Surveillance of Public Space: CCTV, Street Lighting and Crime Prevention*, Crime Prevention Studies, Vol. 10. Monsey, NY: Criminal Justice Press.

17   Mazerolle, L., Hurley, D.C. and Chamlin, M. (2000) *Social Behavior in Public Space: An Analysis of Behavioral Adaptations to CCTV*. Brisbane: Griffith University.

18   Farrington, D.P., Bennett, T.H. and Welsh, B.C. (2002) Rigorous Evaluations of the Effects of CCTV on Crime, unpublished manuscript. Cambridge: Institute of Criminology, University of Cambridge.

19   In the summer of 2003 CCTV will also be introduced into a notorious part of the old city centre: the Red Light District with its drug trading, drug use and prostitution. Because the research design with two sweeps of surveys will be used here as well, results from that evaluation will not be available until 2005.

20   Flight, S. and Van Heerwaarden, Y. (DSP-groep) (2003) *Evaluatie cameratoezicht Amsterdam: effectmeting August Allebéplein, Belgiëplein en Kraaiennest*. Amsterdam: DSP-groep.

21   In Kraaiennest (start of CCTV scheme 1997) and at August Allebéplein the first
      sweep of surveys (June 2001) was conducted after the cameras were installed. In
      the case of August Allebéplein the surveys were conducted a few months after
      the CCTV installation. Therefore, in these two areas, the first sweep of surveys
      cannot be regarded as a proper pre-measurement. Given the possibility that
      CCTV has its biggest effects in the first weeks after installation, the results for
      these two areas have to be interpreted with great care.

22   The number of respondents (inhabitants only) per sweep per location:

August Allebéplein first sweep	126
August Allebéplein second sweep	113
August Allebéplein displacement first sweep	98
August Allebéplein displacement second sweep	117
Belgiëplein first sweep	175
Belgiëplein second sweep	179
Kraaiennest first sweep	96
Kraaiennest second sweep	121

23   'Incivilities' is a concept introduced by Skogan, W.G. and Maxfield, M.G. (1981)
      Coping with Crime, Individual and Neighbourhood Reactions. California: Sage. In
      the surveys in Amsterdam this concept was defined as 'verbal agression' and
      'trouble caused by groups of youngsters'.

24   Note that this square was selected because of its high probability of displacement.
      Therefore the results cannot be generalized to the two other locations, let alone
      to CCTV schemes in general.

25   Note the figures for the scheme starting later (Belgiëplein) show a slightly
      different pattern because by that time the crime trend in the Amsterdam police
      region, the western police district and the police team area was falling, while the
      number of recorded crimes in the CCTV area increased slightly (from 76 the year
      before to 84 the year after: $+8$).

Web resources on CCTV:

Links on CCTV Europe/worldwide: *http://www.e-doca.net/links.htm*
Links on CCTV in the Netherlands: *http://www.e-doca.net/Countries/Europe/Netherlands/
Netherlands.htm*

Chapter 9

The Impact of Monitored CCTV in a Retail Environment: What CCTV Operators Do and Why

Karryn Loveday and Martin Gill[1]

There are a number of features that help explain the effectiveness or lack of effectiveness of CCTV. In this paper we report on research findings from a small-scale study on the impact of CCTV operators in a major retail chain. Our objectives are to understand the role of operators, the work they do, and the broader functions they perform within security departments and store structure. We achieved these by means of observation, supplemented by interviews with operators and other staff. Our findings raised questions about the role of operators and lead us to make some recommendations.

Introduction

The purpose of the research was to gain a perspective into the working lives of CCTV operators. The main purpose was to find out what made them suspicious and why, to understand their actions and the losses they prevent. By understanding what operators did, why they did so and the benefits of having a designated CCTV operator we were able to move on and form an understanding of the impact that having a CCTV operator made to a store and how that impact could be increased. The majority of larger retailers have a CCTV system within their outlets. The question here is not should they have CCTV but how its potential can be maximized by those who monitor it.

This paper will consider what operators did during the course of their shift, who they monitored and explore why they made those choices. Specifically it will consider what causes an operator to become suspicious of an individual and monitor him/her and will take account of an individual's age, behaviour, appearance, social circumstances and ethnicity. How operators weight the risk of shop theft in terms of which areas of a store they monitor the most frequently is also considered. Aspects of the working role and environment of an operator are looked at to gain an understanding of what they consider to have positive and negative impacts on their role. This is followed by a discussion on how the impact of operators could be increased in practical terms.

There is a distinct lack of previous research focusing on what CCTV operators do and why. Norris and Armstrong[2] conducted a large-scale study focusing on who and what CCTV operators look at and why. These writers observed 25 operators, logging the nature of each surveillance made by an operator during the course of their shift resulting in data on 888 targeted surveillances. The control rooms were located within three cities—a large commercial city centre, an affluent county town and a less affluent inner-city location populated with a high minority ethnic community, with each site operating different CCTV technology. This study then complements their work in that it focuses on the retail sector[3] and places less emphasis on observation, instead using a range of different methodologies which are discussed below.

Methodology

This research was commissioned by a major food retailer and focused upon a sample of 17 stores. All of the retail outlets had the same CCTV system installed. They were all of the same brand and specification and all monitored the same areas within the store.[4] Nine of the retail outlets were monitored by designated CCTV operators and the remaining eight were not,[5] giving two samples of stores. This paper concentrates in particular on those stores where CCTV is monitored by designated operators.

The retailer collected its own data relating to the loss and shrinkage each store suffered. However, because of inconsistent collection and recording practice common with this type of data, it could not be relied upon. Not only was there a lack of consistency in how reports were made and how incidents were classified within them, but also whether reports were made at all as this was an issue left to the discretion of individual security officers.

Each sample store was visited during the first stages of the research so that operators and their managers were fully informed as to the nature of the research. This was important as there was a large degree of self-reporting to be undertaken by the operators and it was vital that they fully understood not only how to complete this stage of the research but also why the data were needed. It was also important for the operators to understand that the research was not about identifying 'bad' or 'ineffective' operators who may then be dismissed. During early visits the opportunity was taken to both observe operators at work and understand something of their working environment. This allowed for an insight into their working practices, conditions and perspectives which facilitated the development of a checklist, which the CCTV operators completed at a later stage in the research.

The checklist was used to record details of what each CCTV operator did during his/her shift including data about areas of the retail outlet that were monitored. They used the checklist to log any time that they spent away from monitoring the CCTV system and whether there were any particular positive or negative occurrences during their shift. Where monitoring of an individual led to further action being taken operators were asked to complete a shift incident sheet ('SIS') for each incident.[6] This provided information on what it was about a particular individual that attracted the attention of the operator and made him/her suspicious, for example was he/she a known offender, was it their body language or age, had a member of staff directed the attention of the operator. The operators then logged any action taken as a result of monitoring. Sometimes no action was taken, as an offence was not verified; sometimes staff asked for assistance or the police were called.[7] The value of recovered and lost stock was also noted. We were also able to verify the accuracy of the operators' self-reports against the security log and records kept by individual stores and compiled by the security manager.

All CCTV operators were interviewed about their working practices, and their views on their role and position within the organization. It was also possible to observe them at work and to introduce them to the checklist and SIS to be sure that they understood them fully. Each operator was observed for at least one six to eight hour shift. This also provided an opportunity to assess the working conditions of CCTV operators. This was instructive as in one case poor lighting interfered with their ability to properly view the monitors. Finally, interviews were conducted with employees who were in some way involved in some aspect of the functioning of CCTV. This included 12 store managers, 13 middle managers and 17 security officers at both monitored and unmonitored stores. It should be stressed that this is a small-scale project of just one retailer, but it is hoped that the findings are instructive.

What CCTV operators do and why

CCTV operators who took part in this study came from predominately non-security backgrounds. In fact the majority were previously employed by the retailer in different roles (typically as shopfloor workers in high-risk and high-value departments where shop theft was considered to be more prevalent), with only two coming from outside the organization, one of these being a former police officer.

We began then by considering what CCTV operators do during their working shift and why. Only four of the 12 CCTV operators interviewed for this research were employed full time. The number of hours a CCTV operator worked was determined by the amount of money store managers could redirect from other budget headings as there was no specific budget for the security department (itself a telling finding). Weekly working hours were allotted on a rota in the case of seven of the 12 operators. The operators believed that by varying their shift patterns shop thieves would be denied the comfort of knowing when they were most likely to be monitored. Nevertheless they held views about the times when thieves were most active and liked to ensure CCTV was monitored where possible in these periods. Certainly one store security officer held the view that thieves had discovered when the part-time operator was off duty in that he noticed more known 'faces' on the operator's rest days. His judgment was that offenders were targeting the store when they knew they would be less likely to be monitored. As a response, the shift patterns of the operator were varied and the capture rate increased. In fact there was a range of other reasons why effectiveness went up but interviewees viewed the effective deployment of a CCTV operator as at least a contributory reason. Indeed, where operators' shifts varied they identified 16.4 theft incidents per shift compared to 4.4 per where shifts were fixed.[8]

Operators were asked whether there was a particular focus or task for their shift so that it was possible to consider whether this had a bearing on the volume of shop thieves identified. In some cases operators were asked to monitor only specific parts of the store or were tasked with reviewing tapes for evidence required by the police, therefore they were not always given a free hand to monitor as they saw fit.

In 87 per cent (184) of shifts operators were given specific tasks to undertake and in just under half (47 per cent) of all shifts operators were given tasks which took them away from monitoring the CCTV system.[9] Table 1 shows the tasks and focuses that operators were given during the research period. In 19 per cent (40) of shifts the operator's time was directed to CCTV system tape management and logging and in 14 per cent of shifts they were required to undertake the role of security officer. There are significant risks attached to operators performing the security officer role—most importantly this is not a role for which they had received formal training. At the time of the research one operator was undertaking the security officer's role on a full-time basis as the only 'security officer' attached to the store. This operator had not received training for either the role of CCTV operator or security officer. Operators reported that in 16 per cent (33) of cases they monitored a particular department and in 10 per cent (21) of shifts their focus was to 'detect crime'.

Car park observation was a low priority mainly because operators associated job success with catching shop thieves and this is not where they are active, and

Table 1. Focus to CCTV operators' shift

Shift focus	Number	Percentage of shifts
Tape logging	40	19%
Monitor particular department	33	16%
Perform role and duties of security officer	29	14%
Administration	27	13%
Detect crime	21	10%
Staff surveillance	20	9%
Car park observations	11	5%
Other	3	1%

in any event they were rarely directed to focus on car parks by management. One perceived 'soft' benefit of CCTV identified by the retailer was that by monitoring the car park customers may well feel safer about leaving their vehicle unattended and, also, visiting the stores late at night. More research is needed to test whether this view is true but the practice was very much on targeting thieves and any other strategies would need to be integrated in a systematic way.

Analysis showed that where operators were left to monitor systems without other duties more shop theft incidents were discovered which led to further action such as an arrest. There are two elements at play here. Firstly, where an operator is not distracted from monitoring they are more successful, and so the finding noted above that monitoring in almost half of all shifts was disturbed is telling. Trust was common where there was a good relationship between operators and the security team in-store. Gerrard[10] also picks up on this point, noting that the police need confidence in the ability of operators to act on their advice.

Operators and suspicion

A CCTV operator's task was to observe individuals and identify who is in the process of or about to commit a criminal act (theft in this case); in other words they had to spot criminals and focus on them. Identifying who is suspicious is under-researched within criminology, although it is recognized that there are different types of suspicion.[11]

When completing the SIS, operators were asked to indicate what it was about the individual that had made them suspicious.[12] The full range of reported

Table 2. Reported causes for suspicion by CCTV operators

Reported causes for suspicion	Number	Percentage of incidents
Behaviour	76	55%
Appearance	47	34%
Body language	47	34%
Notified by other member of staff	47	34%
Looking at high-risk goods	39	28%
Age	29	21%
Known offender	23	17%
Part of a gang	16	12%
Notified by out-of-store security	4	3%
Looking at cameras	11	8%
Ethnicity	4	3%
Single mother	4	3%
Other	6	4%

causes for suspicion are listed in Table 2. It is encouraging to note that behaviour was the most common base for suspicion while body language was among the next most commonly cited reasons.

When asked during interviews to describe in their own words suspicious body language the most frequent type of response noted by a half of operators was acting 'outside of normal shopping behaviour'. This was broken down into walking faster than normal, looking over their shoulder frequently, appearing to have an increased awareness of other people around them, looking at or for cameras and moving to areas of the store where cameras could not view them at all or had only a restricted view. While behaviours that were suspicious included the repeat selection and rejection of items, looking at other shoppers, waiting until the aisle was empty before making a product selection, not inspecting higher value goods before making a selection or multiple selection of the same item. As Table 2 shows, it is instructive that suspicion was in part often generated by 'looking at high-risk goods' or being part of a gang or group. Operators also noted that few offenders would steal while 'shopping' for many items. It was considered more likely that an offender would enter the store, select what they intended to steal and leave. Another indicator was selecting a large amount of items of high value in a trolley, which could then be pushed out of the store without payment.

Suspicion was sometimes generated by appearance. During interviews, operators were asked about what made them suspicious. Key questions of interest included noting whether suspicion was based on training that some (but not all) operators had received, whether they thought in terms of offender stereotypes and the extent to which this influenced the way they monitored. Norris and Armstrong (1999, p. 164) identified young men, and particularly young black men, as being more likely to be monitored by CCTV operators who they typically referred to as 'scrotes', 'scumbags' and 'crapheads'. While ethnicity was not a common trigger for monitoring within this study (see below), the disproportionate focus on young men certainly was and the language operators used to describe them was similar too.

Operators were asked to describe someone who would typically attract their attention. Responses fell into two categories. Eight operators described what they thought a typical offender looked like and the type of individual they monitor most frequently. Males within the age group of 16 to mid twenties (with a maximum age range of 30) wearing sports clothing and of unkempt appearance were described by all eight operators.

> A typical person would be probably below 30, would not have clean shoes, always wear trainers and baggy jeans ... be unshaven and not look particularly clean ... would never wear a suit—look at the lower classes. (CCTV operator 1)

> ... wearing a baseball cap ... scruffy ... young male about mid twenties ... (CCTV operator 2)

However, four of the 12 operators said that they did not feel it was possible to describe a typical person who they would monitor. All four reported that they had received training about good practice in monitoring and all four recorded the detection of more shop thieves. For this quartet, everyone was a potential suspect:

> Can I describe a typical person? I think that is really hard—they are so different. (CCTV operator 3)

> ... could be scruffy or could be clean shaven and everyone wears a baseball cap now. (CCTV operator 4)

> No, it's all people. (CCTV operator 5)

While clearly there is a need for caution about the low numbers here, the results of those operators who did not stereotype offenders were better than those who did. Operators who did stereotype justified their view by pointing to the fact that they caught shop thieves who met their description, but, of course, there was less opportunity to catch different types of shop thieves. Even though some stereotyping operators did have success in spotting shop thieves (and some did not) they identified fewer than non-stereotyping operators.

An operator's suspicion leading to monitoring of a suspected shop thief did not always lead to the witnessing of an actual theft. In 26 per cent of SIS cases it was reported that no offence was committed—the suspect stole nothing and was a 'normal' customer. In 26 per cent (37) of cases the suspicion of the operator led to the incident being described as 'deterred'.[13] Where the monitoring led to a further course of action other members of staff were called on for assistance in 19 per cent (26) of cases, the police were called in 26 per cent (37) of cases and arrests were made in 19 per cent (27). This further action led to stock being recovered in 81 per cent (67) of incident reports and lost in 19 per cent (16).

Having considered who operators watch, the research also looked at the frequency of monitoring by each operator. Operators were asked to indicate how many times in a shift they monitored a suspect and then indicate how many times any such monitoring led to further action being required.

Those monitoring instances where further action was or was not required to be taken are shown in Table 3.

Table 3. Volume monitored against action required

Number of individuals monitored in a shift	Number of times further action was required
0 to 5	20
6 to 10	23
11 to 15	14
16 to 20	18
21 to 25	2
26 to 30	0
31 to 35	0

Where operators monitor a lower number of suspects they appear to produce more results, that is they monitored more individuals where intervention (further action) was required. This finding may be due to the fact that some operators monitored a higher number of individuals because their time was not monopolized monitoring a shop thief. Issues such as knowledge of the local 'faces' meant that identification of suspect shop thieves was easier, resulting in the monitoring of fewer individuals. This is an interesting finding which would benefit from further research.

When the monitoring patterns and successes of operators who had received training were considered, more captures of shop thieves were evident and there was less random or routine monitoring. Operators who had received training discovered 75 per cent (103) of the incidents where further action was taken as a result of their monitoring. One other observation made by operators, which merits more research, was that they felt that it was easier to concentrate on the monitors when they were busy; quietness and boredom appear closely associated.

Having considered why operators monitor someone and how frequently they select different individuals for monitoring (see Tables 2 and 3) we turned to which areas of the retail outlet receive the most monitoring attention (Table 4).

It was noted above that some areas of the store are perceived as more likely targets for theft. As part of the checklist completion, operators were asked to identify how frequently they monitored each department during the course of their shift and the findings are illustrated in Table 4.

In 151 shifts, the Beer, Wines and Spirits department was monitored 30 times or more. Both operators and security officers commented during interview that problems had been experienced with bottle tags being cut off[14] and consequently the department received even more monitoring attention than usual although it always attracted a lot of operators' attention. There is some evidence in the order of departments listed here to support the view of those who have studied shop theft that thieves favour portable items that can easily be sold on.[15]

Measuring the loss prevention in terms of the value of stock recovered, as well as that which was prevented and/or deterred from being taken, is one way in which the effectiveness of an operator can be measured. Where stock was recorded as failed to be recovered, the highest value was between £101 and £200. However, where stock was recovered, the highest value was over £500. During the three-month research period the 12 operators reported recovering £7,447.30 in total. Although the Security Department was not considered to be revenue-generating it clearly did have a contribution to make to profits.

Positive and negative aspects of the shift

The research also gathered data on circumstances and situations which the operators felt had a positive or negative impact upon their shift. It was intended that this would highlight recurrent issues which could be encouraged if they produced a positive influence and addressed if the influence was negative.

In 22 per cent (26) of shifts, operators identified circumstances which they felt had made their shift positive and these are illustrated in Table 5.[16] Where a positive effect was reported for the shift the most common reason was that the CCTV operator had 'made a capture'—they had caught a shop thief. The next

Table 4. Frequency of monitoring different departments by shifts

Department	Never 0	Rarely 1–10	Sometimes 11–20	Often 21–30	A lot 30+
Beers/wines/spirits	4	4	0	19	151
Electrical	4	1	7	28	135
Music & Video	4	2	14	33	119
Main Entrance	4	14	46	57	53
Toiletries/cosmetics	6	17	40	51	53
Meat	10	36	29	36	42
Toys	11	56	16	34	40
Confectionery	7	41	55	26	25
Tobacco Kiosk	13	55	52	22	23
Delicatessen	22	49	30	30	20
Home Decorating	10	40	15	16	14
Checkouts	5	25	60	77	12
Tea/coffee	5	36	47	23	12
Warehouse	15	52	30	24	9
Loading Bay	34	66	2	25	8
Clothing	4	7	24	5	7
Petrol	12	59	12	11	7
Opticians	18	17	17	7	3
Staff entrance	25	79	45	23	3
Restaurant	13	72	30	10	4
Cash office	15	89	47	23	2
Pharmacy	1	41	22	18	0

most frequently commented positive effect (and following on from the first) was the operator having their work recognized—in 15 per cent (7) of cases. Examples of positive comments from operators include:

> We had a police visit today and they told us how impressed with our department they were. This made us all feel positive. (CCTV operator 4)

> I had a positive shift as a lady who had had some money stolen from her came into the office to thank us for our work and gave us a present. This made me feel encouraged about my work. (CCTV operator 2)

However, only four of the store managers communicated the successes of their CCTV operator to other store employees.

Table 5. Positive elements of operators' shifts

Positives	Number of shifts	Percentage of shifts producing positive comments	Percentage of all shifts
Capture of shop thief	25	54%	12%
Work recognized	7	15%	3%
Assistance available to help with duties	6	13%	3%
Deterred theft	4	9%	2%
CCTV system working well	3	6%	1%
Liaison with security from other stores working well	1	2%	0.4%

In 49 per cent (103) of the 211 shifts incorporated in this study, operators reported that there were circumstances that made their job difficult to perform. The most frequent reason given was that of camera failure in 24 per cent (25) of cases. This meant that in 12 per cent of all shifts camera failure was an issue. The positioning of advertising suspended from the ceiling within the store accounted for 20 per cent (21) of the difficulties identified (10 per cent of all shifts) as this obstructed camera views. When all comments concerned with the CCTV equipment were calculated, this accounted for 39 per cent (40) of all difficulties reported (19 per cent of all shifts).

Camera and CCTV system failures were a factor in 22 per cent (11) of negative shifts. During interviews when operators were asked whether there was anything they would 'wish' for to improve their role, the most frequent 'wish' was for camera failures to be rectified more quickly, as identified by five operators, second only to the removal of large advertising and displays which limited their ability to observe customers and stock. In response to the research findings the supermarket chain reassessed the maintenance of the camera systems and through the development of a joint venture now has response times of eight hours for every store and four hours for high-risk stores to rectify camera system failures. A full list of factors which made the operators feel negative about a shift are detailed in Table 6.

In 46 per cent (23) of shifts, operators felt negative about their work, most commonly because no captures were made. This again supports the finding that operators most often measured their job satisfaction by whether they have caught a shop thief. Examples of negative comments from operators include:

Despite intensive obs [observations], no arrests—NEGATIVE. (CCTV operator 7)

Again no offences detected. (CCTV operator 1)

Table 6. Negative elements of operators' shifts

Negatives	Number of shifts	Percentage of shifts producing negative comments	Percentage of all shifts
No captures of shop thieves	23	46%	11%
Camera failure	11	22%	5%
CCTV system failure	8	16%	4%
Camera views blocked	5	10%	2%
No assistance available to help with duties	3	6%	1%

The type of relationships operators developed with other employees and external agencies such as the police contributed to their reflections on the shift. A good relationship between security officers and CCTV operators, one based on trust, will increase their efficiency. The working relationship between security officers and CCTV operators is that the security officers frequently detain a suspect on the information provided by the CCTV operator (by radio and telephone). Security officers sometimes arrest solely on the information provided by the operator, not having witnessed the incident themselves. If the information was inaccurate there would be the risk of legal repercussions for the security officer/company and/or the store. This is a major issue and one that will be revisited in the discussion. Effective training, coupled with 'a few good captures' were the foundation on which trust was built:

> There are not many people in this world I would trust to do that [be accurate in detecting shop thieves] so he has to be a very very special person. He has to win my trust for a start off. (Security officer)

One of the most positive findings to emerge from this research was the impact that the designated CCTV operators had on the awareness of and attitudes towards security issues held by other employees within the store in that a designated CCTV operator appeared to generate greater awareness of security issues among colleagues. It was pointed out to the research team that employees on the shopfloor felt more confident about providing information to the security department where a designated CCTV operator was in place as the security team were more able to respond immediately. Shopfloor colleagues supplied CCTV operators with information about a suspicious individual in 29 per cent of cases where further action was required. Within monitored stores, shopfloor employees discovered the same amount of incidents as security officers—41 per cent.

During interviews, the issue of operators having an influence on the stores' relationship with local police was explored. In monitored stores this relationship was reported to have been enhanced by the store having an operator, not least because there was potentially evidence that could be useful to them readily available. In some cases the police used store car parks as a base from which to conduct covert surveillance and observation of known offenders. While such police investigations were not typically connected to shop theft the operator played a key role in helping monitor those under surveillance—it was an additional benefit.

Not all stores benefited from local police having a positive attitude towards monitored CCTV. One store reported that their local force had threatened to withdraw response from the store if their CCTV system was monitored. The police felt that they were unable to cope with an increase in arrests from the store. This is an emerging problem in policing—technology is good but personnel are still needed to back it up.

One other aspect of a shift that emerged as negative during interviews and observation periods was the working conditions. Workstations are typically small with temperature and lighting problems. At no workstation could the lighting be adequately controlled by the operator—other than by the provision of lamps—and the glare of the overhead lighting often made monitoring difficult. Moreover, operators lamented that they were frequently either too warm or too cold (some operators wore their outdoor coats at work). Operators described the room temperature as too warm in seven of the 11 monitored sites.

Discussion

This research, commissioned by a major food retailer, was a small-scale study. This paper focused on the findings relating to nine stores with designated CCTV operators utilizing the same CCTV system. Having considered during the research what CCTV operators did and why and the impact of having a designated operator to monitor the CCTV system it was found that there were several ways in which the impact of utilizing such an operator would be increased. It is to this issue—increasing that impact—that we now turn.

The evidence suggests that stores with designated CCTV operators generate more benefits to the security of a store. This is reflected in the fact that stores where the CCTV system was monitored by a designated operator benefited from a higher theft discovery rate, together with a higher stock recovery rate and, consequently, reduced loss. A designated CCTV operator also provided a more accessible focal point for security for all colleagues within the store. Indeed, the research identified that there were opportunities to improve the visibility of a CCTV operator's impact on loss. Here the key issues are the training and time management of the operators.

One of the most obvious ways of increasing the impact of operators' work is via the provision of training. Yet, when asked, four untrained operators felt that the role was not one people could really be trained for—spotting potential shop thieves was considered to be instinctive.

> The reason they asked me to do this was because I have this gut instinct about people . . . I can just pick it up. (CCTV operator 8)

Only six of the 12 operators had reported receiving training when they started their role—in all of these cases training was given by their security officer. A formalized dedicated training system did not exist. Only a quarter of operators had been advised by anyone as to what they should look out for while monitoring. When asked about training provided, typical responses included:

> I've done a bit of computing and that and it's basically the same system really. (CCTV operator 9)

> Just play around a bit and learn for yourself how it worked and they [the security officers] have shown me as I needed it. (CCTV operator 1)

However, two operators reported that they had received training from their security manager which took the form of reviewing past incidents on tape. Here, tapes of past incidents would be reviewed and then stopped at various stages of the incident with a discussion as to 'what happens next', 'what action should be taken next' and a review of both positive and negative outcomes to particular actions. This form of training was explained to the researcher in positive terms.

> It helped me know what I was looking for and how important it was to learn the layout of the store to keep continuity when you are following someone on the camera. (CCTV operator 5)

This is certainly an area that merits attention. As noted above, negative comments about a shift were often closely associated with a feeling that monitoring had failed. As a response to the findings of the research the supermarket chain formalized the role of CCTV operator by providing a budget for the role in approximately two-thirds of stores. This formalization of the role also provides a job description and standardized training for operators.

Another possibility for increasing the impact of CCTV operators is that of utilizing the knowledge and intelligence gathered by them. The method employed by the retailer to collect stock loss reports did not support the attachment of images from the CCTV system. Not being able to share images with local stores meant much of the intelligence gathered by security officers and CCTV operators was not fully utilized. An image gives much more information than a description—picking out the exact white, male, 32 years, tall with dark hair in a crowded supermarket is not easy.

If password-protected sites were made available to local stores they could post images of, for example, repeat offenders or refunders stealing in their area.[17] Depending on the volume and the capacity of any potential intranet site, images of banned offenders could be stored so that if they were to (and they do) offend in another store they could be charged with the more serious offence of burglary—perhaps acting as more of a deterrent than flouting a ban.

Communication between security departments in local stores was described as 'informal'. There did not appear to be formal links or procedures for security officers and CCTV operators to gather and discuss themes and trends occurring in their area and the activities of particular offenders who are known to offend in more than one store. By sharing information, the effectiveness and impact of the CCTV system could have been increased. An offender who was operating in one store, who paid a visit to another operator's store, would not do so anonymously.

In fact, the supermarket chain took up these recommendation from the research and now have a password-protected intelligence site within their own intranet system. This allows for the viewing of images of offenders and the exchange of information with positive results. For example, tagging guns were stolen from a store by offenders and were then used to steal clothing from 21 stores and return the items for fraudulent refunds. As a result of the information shared on the intranet site the offenders were caught eight days later by an in-store security officer who had viewed their images on the intranet site.

Notes

1   Karryn Loveday is the Crime and Disorder Officer for the Safer Middlesborough Partnership; email karryn_loveday@middlesborough.gov.uk. Professor Martin Gill is Director of Perpetuity Research and Consultancy International (PRCI) Ltd and a Professor of Criminology at the University of Leicester; email m.gill@perpetuitygroup.com. The authors would like to thank Jenna Allen, Tricia Jessiman, Mike McCahill, Clive Norris and Daniel Swain for their comments on an early draft of this paper.

2   Norris, C. and Armstrong, G. (1999) *The Maximum Surveillance Society: The Rise of Closed Circuit Television*. Oxford: Berg.

3   There is very little research on the use of CCTV in the retail sector. But for exceptions see Beck, A. and Willis A. (1995) *Crime and Security: Managing the Risk to Safe Shopping*. Leicester: Perpetuity Press; McCahill, M. (2002) *The Surveillance Web*. Cullompton: Willan; also Gill, M. and Turbin, V. (1999) Evaluating 'Realistic Evaluation': Evidence from a Study of CCTV, in Painter, K. and Tilley, N. (eds), *Surveillance of Public Space: CCTV, Street Lighting and Crime Prevention*, Crime Prevention Studies, Vol. 10., Monsey, NY: Criminal Justice Press; Gill, M.L. and Turbin, V. (1998) CCTV and Shop Theft: Towards a Realistic Evaluation, in Norris, C., Armstrong, G. and Moran, J. (eds), *Surveillance, Order and Social Control*. Aldershot: Gower. Also, Norris, C. and McCahill, M. (2003) *On the Threshold to the Urban Panopticon: Analysing the Employment of Closed Circuit Television (CCTV) in European Cities and Assessing Its Social and Political Impacts*, Centre for Criminology and Criminal Justice, University of Hull Working Paper.

4   Not each CCTV system contained the same number of cameras but they were all able to use the standard departmental checklist for recording their monitoring activity.

5   Monitoring in these outlets did take place on an ad hoc basis by security staff but no designated CCTV operator was in place.

6   In total 211 checklists and 137 shift incident sheets were completed.

7   It should be noted that an offence was considered to have been 'deterred' when a suspected shop thief either purchased or put down the goods they were carrying and left the store. The researchers cannot assume that a theft would have actually taken place but retain the category 'deterred' to describe the CCTV operators' perception of what had taken place.

8   115 thefts were reported by the seven operators whose hours were varied and 22 by the five operators with fixed hours. All shifts were typically eight hours long.

9   Shifts spent tape logging, performing duties of security officer, administration and 'other' tasks total 46.7 per cent of shifts.

10   See Gerrard, G. (1999) *Public Surveillance CCTV: An Evaluation of the Effectiveness of Local Authority and Police Controlled Systems*. MSc Thesis, University of Cambridge.

11   See, for example, Baldwin, R. and Kinsey, R. (1985) 'Rules, Realism and the Police Act', *Critical Social Policy*, Spring, pp 89–102, who make a distinction between 'particular suspicion' of a specific person in a specific instance; and 'general suspicion', where it is believed there is a better than average chance someone may have committed an offence (p 94).

12   Operators could select from a list as many factors which aroused their suspicion as they wished for each incident. Table 2 shows the number of times each cause of suspicion was selected and then in what percentage of incidents each cause of suspicion was given.

13   It should be noted that an offence was considered to have been 'deterred' when a suspected shop thief either purchased or put down the goods they were carrying and left the store. It cannot be assumed that a theft would have actually taken place, rather that this was the CCTV operator's perception of what had occurred.

14   Security officers expressed concern that shop thieves were arming themselves to remove bottle tags. When asked, they felt that having an operator monitoring them while they apprehended or deterred a shop thief made them feel safer about approaching a potentially armed offender.

15   See Clarke, R.V.G. (2002) *Shoplifting*, Problem-Orientated Guide for Police Series. Washington, DC: US Department of Justice.

16   Operators could identify as many factors as they wished for each shift.

17   The store is of the view that provided these images were stored for a specified period (i.e. not indefinitely) and the site was secure there does not appear to be an obvious conflict with the Data Protection Act.

Chapter 10

An Evaluation of the CCTV Scheme at Oslo Central Railway Station

Stig Winge and Johannes Knutsson[1]

In an evaluation of a CCTV scheme introduced in the centre of Oslo outside the Central Railway Station, effects on public order, criminality and feelings of safety were studied. A significant increase in recorded incidents occurred in the monitored area, indicating an increased detection rate. Among the categories of crime, the only reduction occurred in robbery/theft from persons and possibly in bicycle thefts. Victimization surveys with local business before and after the onset of the scheme indicated small and mostly insignificant changes in perception of criminality, disorder and safety. Respondents still had faith in the effectiveness of the CCTV scheme, but to a lesser extent than before its introduction.

Introduction

Impressed by accounts from police in the UK, Oslo Police Department introduced a trial CCTV scheme in 1999. Politicians in Norway have been reluctant to accept CCTV programmes run by the police. The reason is fear that the privacy of individuals could come under threat. However, should CCTV prove to be effective in reducing crime and increasing feelings of safety, there may be a willingness to reassess this position. Therefore, as a condition for allowing the police to trial CCTV, the scheme had to be evaluated. The research unit at the National Police Academy was asked to carry out this evaluation.

Surveilled area

The zone selected for camera coverage was determined to be the area just outside the Central Railway Station in the heart of Oslo. This area is best characterized as a typical city-centre district with shops, hotels, restaurants and pubs. It includes a large outdoor public square in the vicinity of a transport junction, with bus and tram stops, taxi ranks, parking places, a subway station and, of course, the main railway station. It is estimated that on a daily basis about 70,000 persons pass through the area. The vicinity of the railway station has become a meeting place for drug abusers. The congregation of drug addicts creates a visible and more or less constant problem. It may be expected that the study would encounter and capture both the degree and type of crime as well as problems of social order that exist within the context of a modern city centre.

CCTV scheme

Six cameras are used and operated by a specially trained crew with their operations room located at the Central Station. There are direct links to Oslo police command centre, which means that it is also possible to follow events on TV monitors at dispatch central in headquarters.

The TV cameras provide for a more or less constant supervision of the area, the technique making it possible to detect and follow the development of single episodes from a distance. Information can be continually transmitted to police patrols that may be directed to an ongoing incident and intervene.

Theory

A CCTV scheme may be characterized as a situational measure. The preventive effects are achieved by increasing the risk, effort or moral cost or, by decreasing profits from crime.[2] The preventive effects of CCTV schemes are argued to come about by affecting the risk of detection, as it is subjectively perceived, or through actual risk. More specifically, it is possible to divide active mechanisms into several sub-categories, e.g. 'you will be detected', 'caught in the act' or 'feelings of safety increase natural surveillance since more people are present',[3] which, by using different active components, creates the effect. When analysing such mechanisms, it is of vital importance to understand in what context a given mechanism is effective.[4] However, data necessary to analyse these mechanisms is not provided in this study. The goal is to document effects, irrespective of whether they have come about through increasing the perceived or actual risk.

Earlier research

There are a great number of CCTV schemes in operation around the world. In England, it was estimated that there were more than 400 projects operating in the late 1990s, mainly in city centres.[5] However, only a small fraction of these have been evaluated, and in many cases these evaluations have been carried out by untrained practitioners with vested interests.[6]

During the past few years, however, several evaluations with scientifically acceptable designs, including follow-up periods of more than 12 months, have been carried out. On the whole these studies may be divided into two groups—those that show clear preventive effects and those with mixed results. Three of the nine studies assessed demonstrated reductions in property crimes[7] while the remaining six evaluations showed ambiguous results.[8]

Differences in outcomes are to be expected. These may be due to natural differences in sites, e.g. physical structure, level and type of crime, technology and systems by which surveillance schemes are operated. Also the evaluations themselves have had somewhat different designs and used different types of indicators.

Generally, CCTV appears to be effective when introduced to reduce property crimes in high crime areas where surveillance is targeted to a more limited area.[9] While CCTV does not appear to be effective in reducing violent crimes, there are findings supporting the view that the seriousness of violent crimes decreases.[10] A likely explanation is that patrols can be directed to places where acts of violence occur and intervene. In addition, there is no convincing evidence that displacement effects[11] are natural and unavoidable consequences of CCTV. This result is in accordance with other findings on studies of displacement effects.[12]

Data and methods

In order to answer the two overriding research questions related to effectiveness in reducing crime and increasing feelings of safety, three sub-studies were conducted using different types of data. To study overall preventive effects, studies of incidents and crimes recorded by the police were used. If crimes are reduced in the area covered by CCTV, a possible negative outcome could be a displacement of crime. This effect is examined in the incident log data study. Effects on opinions of crime and disorder as well as on feelings of security were studied in surveys aimed at local business. The three sub-studies are presented below.

Incident log data
When a police patrol is dispatched to a job, or when police officers take initiative on their own to intervene, the incidents are recorded in the police incident log system. In the incident log study, monthly recorded incidents by Oslo Police Department's dispatch centre are used as data; 12 months prior to the start of the CCTV scheme and 12 months after. Information on initiative for intervention, location, time and type of incident is analysed. Incidents are selected from an experimental area, from possible displacement areas and a

control area. As possible displacement areas, zones adjacent to the area covered by cameras were utilized. The rationale for this choice is that these unsurveyed areas are part of the larger locale and, on the whole, used by the public in the same manner as the CCTV area. The selected control area is situated in the city centre of Oslo but away and separate from the experiment area. It lacks some of the characteristics of that area (there is only one railway station in Oslo), although the control area has a large flow of people in both the early and late hours of the day.

In some analyses the indicator is treated as an independent variable (reflecting detection rate) and in some as the dependent variable (reflecting incidents that have occurred). The increased surveillance is supposed to reveal more incidents, and negative consequences following detection will decrease willingness to engage in such activities, and thus lead to fewer incidents.[13]

Recorded crimes

A common indicator of criminality is crimes reported to the police. Besides the problems of unreported crimes, there are other shortcomings. In the Norwegian system it is not possible to pinpoint the location of crimes and there is no information as to whether the crimes occurred indoors or outdoors. The categorization of crimes uses mainly legal categories. In all, it means that this source of information on the whole lacks necessary precision. However, the data was used as a control and it was possible to use it in a meaningful way for at least some categories of crime.

Crimes reported to the police could be geographically located within two sub-areas roughly covering the experimental area. The rest of the precinct where the CCTV scheme is located is used as the control. This means that the control area is not the same as the one used for incident data. Crimes reported for the two years preceding the onset of the surveillance scheme and one year after are analysed on a monthly basis.

There is some overlap between incident log data and recorded crimes. However, a great many incidents do not comprise crimes and crimes may be reported without being recorded in the incident log data system, e.g. when civilians come directly to police stations.

Survey data

In order to be part of the business survey the enterprise had to be located in the experimental area and the premises needed to be on street level with an entrance from the area covered by the CCTV. All local businesses meeting these conditions were visited in order to encourage them to take part in the victim survey. The aim was to obtain senior respondents who had worked in the area for a longer period. The rationale for choosing this group was their intimate knowledge of problems created by crime and disorder. One evaluation of a police intervention on a local problem of social disorder demonstrated that businesses are vulnerable and sensitive to changes in the level of disorder.[14]

The survey centred on opinions about crime (defined as violent crimes, theft and vandalism) and disorder (exemplified as drunkenness, begging, littering and disturbances). Information was also sought regarding possible consequences for the respondent, usually the person in charge of the business, and with regard to the perceived consequences for employees, customers and the business itself. Data was collected on three occasions; the first six months before the onset of the CCTV scheme, the second six months after, and the third after 18 months. Of the 60 businesses fulfilling the necessary requirements, 50 took part in the first survey (response rate 83 per cent).

The second survey was conducted one year after the first. This time interval was chosen to minimize influences of seasonal variations in crime and disorder. However, as the onset of the scheme was delayed (it had only been operative for about six months at that time), a six-month observation period was chosen (instead of 12 months as in the first survey). A rather unanticipated occurrence was that as many as eleven of the 50 businesses participating in the first survey had closed down or moved out and had been replaced by new enterprises. It is our impression that these new enterprises were aiming at a more affluent customer-base, thus indicating that the turnover of businesses is not the result of a 'broken window' syndrome.[15] In the second survey, 33 of the 39 remaining businesses participated (response rate 85 per cent).

The third and final data collection was carried out as a control, to catch long-term effects. However, only results from the first and second collection of data are presented here, as data from the third survey did not indicate any changes in previous results. In addition, the level of participation was low. Of the 50 business enterprises that took part in the first wave, only 18 participated in the third. This is mainly due to the turnover of businesses. Thus a large proportion of local business had not experienced a period without CCTV surveillance at the time of the third collection of data.

Onset of CCTV scheme

It was intended that the programme should start considerably earlier than it did. This delay caused two problems. Firstly, the observation period in the second local business survey became shorter than planned, making the third wave necessary. Secondly, it increased the uncertainty as to when the CCTV surveillance had commenced. The signs informing the public that TV cameras covered the area were in place before the operation started. Intense mass media coverage beforehand also contributed to the confusion.

The issue is crucial, as it has been shown that crime reductions may appear before crime preventive measures are actually put into practice.[16] If eventual effects mainly come about as the consequences of perceptions, it is the perceived time of commencement that is essential. Since it was a totally new scheme with inexperienced personnel it could be argued that it will take some time before the system functions properly. Thus, if it is mainly through actual consequences that the surveillance derives its effects, the vital period is when it starts to run to its full potential. Of course, it could also be the case that different segments of the public, or different types of offences, are affected in various ways. The conclusion is that it is necessary to be flexible and to look for trends and changes both prior to and after the period when CCTV systems commence.

Results

Incident log data study
After the start of the programme, an increase of 35.5 per cent in recorded incidents was observed in the experimental area, as was a small but insignificant increase in both the control and displacement areas (Table 1). An analysis of trends (not shown here) revealed that the increase in the experimental area began some months after the start of the CCTV scheme. The findings indicate that the risk of detection has increased in the experimental area due to the CCTV programme.

Table 1. Number of recorded incidents before and after onset of CCTV scheme, by type of area

Area	12 months before	12 months after	Difference	Change %	t-test
Experiment	1,102	1,491	+389	+35.3	***
Control	388	399	+11	+2.8	n.s.
Displacement	410	413	+3	+0.7	n.s.

***Significant at the 0.01 level, n.s. not significant.

In order to interpret the results, it is necessary to understand the processes behind the recording of incidents. One important aspect is the reason for an incident being brought to the attention of the police, that is whether it was the police themselves (proactive) or a member of general public (reactive).

The pattern is clear—in the experimental area the number of proactive incidents increased considerably (Table 2). The reason is not only the more intense surveillance because of CCTV, but incidents where officers took the initiative themselves accounted for more than half of the increase.

Table 2. Number of recorded incidents by area and initiative before and change after onset of CCTV scheme

Area	Police (proactive)			Public (reactive)		
	Before	Change	%	Before	Change	%
Experiment	564	+461	+82.0	465	−90	−19.4
Control	164	−29	−17.7	181	+40	+22.1
Displacement	114	−25	−21.9	252	+28	+13.5

A possible explanation for the decrease in citizen-initiated interventions (reactive) in the experimental area is that police are now detecting incidents that without TV surveillance would only have come to the attention of the public.

In both the control and displacement areas the outcome is reversed with fewer interventions on the initiative of the police and more by citizens. The decrease in proactive incidents in both the control and displacement areas and the proportion of the increase in the experimental area could be due to a police displacement effect. Officers may find it more rewarding to operate in the experimental area, since they can work more purposefully guided by information from the CCTV crew, an explanation supported by the officer in charge of the operation.

Furthermore, it is necessary to break down incidents into type of event. Analyses show that significant changes have occurred in the experimental area for only three types of incident. Recorded incidents of violence and narcotic offences increased while robberies/theft from persons decreased. In the experimental area no difference was detected in incidents concerning public order. There were no significant changes for any type of incident in either the control or displacement areas (Table 3).

The increase in recorded acts of violence in the experimental area is explained by the growth of police-initiated incidents, which is larger than the decrease in incidents brought to their attention by citizens, thus representing an overall increase in the detection rate. Thus it is argued that a larger proportion of the acts of violence will be recorded as a consequence of the CCTV surveillance. An analysis of the trends (not shown here) shows that an increasing trend before onset changed to a less intense increase after. In all, this points to a positive development in the experimental area. However, it is unclear how it is related to the CCTV scheme.

There has been a marked increase in recorded narcotics offences—from 269 to 503. This is in all likelihood a result of increased opportunities to detect and

Table 3. Number of recorded incidents by area and type of incident before and change (%) after onset of CCTV scheme

	Violence		Public order		Narcotics		Robbery/theft from person	
	Before	Change	Before	Change	Before	Change	Before	Change
Experiment	204	+26.0 **	402	+10.4 n.s.	269	+87.0 ***	133	−26.3 *
Displacement	137	+4.4 n.s.	156	+1.3 n.s.	16	(−50.0) n.s.	20	+35.0 n.s.
Control	98	+14.3 n.s.	145	+3.4 n.s.	41	−2.4 n.s.	30	−3.3 n.s.

T-tests: ***Significant at the 0.01 level; **0.05 level; *0.1 level, n.s. not significant.

intervene in the drug scene, thus accounting for a rise in the detection rate. The number of incidents is very small in the control and displacement area both before and after onset. The data indicates that a drug scene has been located in the experimental area and still exists there.

The only registered significant decrease is for robbery/theft from persons. Prior to the onset of the CCTV programme, 133 incidents were recorded and 98 after, constituting a decrease of 26 per cent. The non-significant 35 per cent increase in robbery/theft from person in the control area, involved seven more incidents. In the displacement area there was one incident less (30 vs. 29). Together this information indicates a decrease that could be attributed to the camera surveillance with no detected displacement.

The recorded crimes study
Earlier it was stated that the nature of recorded crime data makes it less useful for the purposes of this evaluation. There are no significant changes for narcotics offences, grand theft, simple theft and car theft in the experimental area compared with the two years preceding the introduction of CCTV. Acts of violence increased significantly. This growth, however, occurred two years before the CCTV scheme was implemented. In the years prior to and following the first year of CCTV coverage, levels of reported acts of violence were similar. In fact, due to more acts being detected by the police, a decrease could hardly be expected in the number of recorded crimes of violence.

Two types of crime show significant reductions: theft from cars (66.5[17] vs. 42) and bicycle thefts (39.5 vs. 28). As regards theft from cars, there has been a considerable reduction in the number of available parking spaces, thus making a change in the opportunity structure the most probable explanation. In the control area, there was a minor decrease in bicycle thefts—a 3.3 per cent reduction (1,401 vs. 1,321) compared to a 29.1 per cent decrease in the experimental area. With respect to bicycle theft and considering the visible way in which they are stolen, it cannot be ruled out that the CCTV scheme is responsible for the decline.

Local business surveys
About 20 per cent of respondents considered crime to be a 'great' or a 'very great' problem for them. No change in perceptions is indicated between the situations before and after the introduction of CCTV. Problems created by crime for employees, customers and, to a larger degree, for businesses, were assessed as greater than for respondents themselves. None of the differences between the two data collection periods were significant[18] for any group (Figure 1).

Figure 1. Perception of crime as creating a great or very great problem last 12 months (1999) or last 6 months (2000), prior to introduction of CCTV scheme and after, according to category (n.s. = non-significant difference)

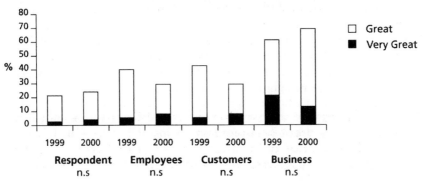

As a follow-up, a question was asked as to whether any changes in crime had taken place. About 20 per cent of respondents in the second survey stated that a change for the better had occurred, thus possibly indicating an effect of CCTV surveillance. However, about the same proportion of respondents gave the same response before the introduction of the CCTV scheme. The only category for which there is a significant difference is employees. Respondents perceived that the crime situation for their employees had changed for the better after the introduction of the CCTV scheme (Figure 2).

It should be pointed out that there is not necessarily a contradiction between perceiving a problem as decreasing but still recognizing it as substantial.

On the whole, problems created by disturbances of public order were considered to be of greater magnitude for all categories except for business, than problems

Figure 2. Perception of changes (for the better or much for the better) in crime last 12 months (1999) or last 6 months (2000), prior to introduction of CCTV scheme and after, according to category (n.s. = non-significant difference)

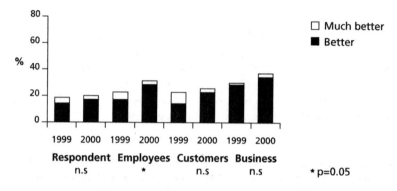

created by crime. Although there were decreases in the proportion of respondents who perceived the situation of public order to be a 'great' or 'very great' problem, the reduction is not significant. The pattern is similar for the way in which problems of public order were perceived to affect both employees and customers—reductions that nevertheless were not significant. Problems for businesses were assessed to be greater after the onset of the CCTV scheme, although this change was not significant (Figure 3).

Figure 3. Perception of disturbances of public order as creating a great or very great problem last 12 months (1999) or last 6 months (2000), prior to introduction of CCTV scheme and after, according to category (n.s. = non-significant difference)

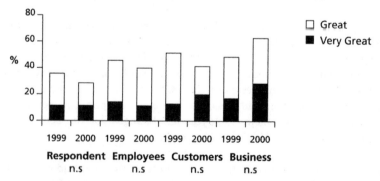

However, respondents experienced a change for the better in the situation concerning public order, a change that is statistically significant for all categories (Figure 4).

Figure 4. Perception of changes (for the better or much for the better) in public order last 12 months (1999) or last 6 months (2000), prior to introduction of CCTV scheme and after, according to category

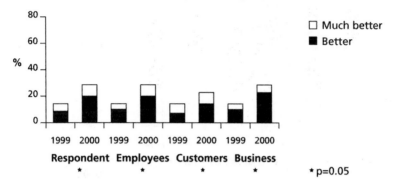

The proportion of respondents who themselves considered that the situation had changed for the 'better', or 'much better', increased from about 13 per cent to about 27 per cent. Except for the customer category, the perceived difference in change was of about the same magnitude.

Almost all respondents had a positive attitude towards CCTV. Eighty-four per cent were content with plans to introduce a police-operated scheme, and 80 per cent were satisfied once it was in operation. Only a small fraction considered supervision by cameras to create a problem for their personal privacy. Rather, a large majority—over 80 per cent—in both surveys indicated that privacy was not threatened at all or only to a small degree. Results are in accordance with findings from other studies.[19]

However, faith in the effectiveness of the CCTV declined. Before the CCTV scheme was introduced, nearly 70 per cent believed that to a high degree it would contribute to reducing crime. More than 60 per cent believed that it would substantially decrease disturbances of public order and about two-thirds believed that it would increase feelings of safety to a considerable degree (Figure 5). Most likely, the high expectations were created by the way the CCTV was portrayed in the mass media, combined with the fact that it was run by the police—an institution the public has great trust in.

While the majority still had confidence in the positive effects after implementation of the scheme, it was not as firm as previously. Rates decreased significantly for all items to about one-third who strongly believed in the effectiveness of CCTV. This particular result could be seen as a kind of validation of the results presented above. Respondents' expectations were simply not met by their own experiences.

Figure 5. Respondents beliefs in effectiveness of CCTV to achieve less crime, less disturbances of public order and greater safety, prior to introduction of CCTV scheme and after

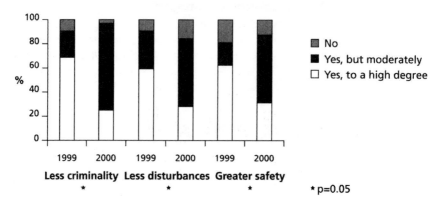

Conclusion

The main results of the evaluation may be summarized as follows:

- More incidents were detected in the experimental area. Data indicates that this is a result of the implementation of the CCTV scheme and to some extent of more officers patrolling the area.

- There are indications of reductions in two types of crimes; robbery/theft from persons and bicycle thefts.

- Surveys of local business showed small and, in almost all cases, insignificant changes in the perception of crime and public order. However, more indicated that they perceived a change for the better in terms of public order.

- Most respondents had positive attitudes towards CCTV, but confidence in its effectiveness declined.

The Oslo police force had great faith in CCTV when it was introduced. However, the evaluation could not document any straightforward strong effects on criminality, public order or feelings of safety. It still remains to be seen whether the programme will be abolished, continue as before or be enlarged. Hopefully the evaluation will have contributed to more informed discussions about CCTV.

The result is in line with evaluations of CCTV schemes in other city centres. In a systematic review of evaluations, it was found that in city settings and public housing, CCTV led to a negligible reduction of crimes in the experimental area compared with the control areas, and that CCTV seems to be most effective in reducing car theft and theft from cars in car parks.[20]

In future research some critical issues remain to be examined. To understand the mechanisms that operate, it would be crucial to determine the relative importance of perceived and actual risk and their relationship. The rationale is that the expected effects of CCTV are ultimately supposed to be achieved by an increased risk of being detected while engaging in unwanted behaviour.

Notes

1   Stig Winge is an advisor at the Norwegian National Police Directorate and Johannes Knutsson is a professor and director of research at the National Police Academy, Norway. E-mail: johannes.knutsson@phs.no.

2   See, for instance, Clarke, R.V. (ed.) (1997) *Situational Crime Prevention: Successful Case Studies*. New York: Harrow & Heston.

3   Tilley, N. (1998) Evaluating the Effectiveness of CCTV Schemes, in Norris, C., Moran, J. and Armstrong, G. (eds), *Surveillance, Closed Circuit Television and Social Control*. Aldershot: Ashgate, pp 139–153.

4   Pawson, R. and Tilley, N. (1997) *Realistic Evaluation*. London: Sage.

5   Painter, K. and Tilley, N. (eds) (1999) *Surveillance of Public Space: CCTV, Street Lighting and Crime Prevention*, Crime Prevention Studies, Vol. 10. Monsey NY: Criminal Justice Press.

6   Pawson, R. and Tilley, N. (1994) What works in Evaluation Research?, *British Journal of Criminology*, Vol. 34, No. 3, pp 291–306.

7   Brown, B. (1995) *CCTV in Town Centres: Three Case Studies*, Police Research Group Crime Detection and Prevention Series Paper No. 68. London: Home Office; Short, E. and Ditton, J. (1996) *Does Closed Circuit Television Prevent Crime? An Evaluation of the use of CCTV Surrveillance Cameras in Airdrie Town Centre*. Edinburgh: Scottish Office Central Research Unit; Armitage, R., Smyth R. and Pease, K. (1999) Burnley CCTV Evaluation, in Painter and Tilley (1999), op. cit., pp 225–51. (Actually in Brown's study three schemes were evaluated and positive results were found in one of the sites.)

8   Brown, op. cit.; Skinns, D. (1998) Crime Reduction, Diffusion and Displacement: Evaluating the Effectiveness of CCTV, in Norris *et al.*, op. cit., pp 175–88; Ditton, J., Short, E., Phillips, S., Norris, C. and Armstrong, G. (1999) *The Effect of Closed Circuit Television on Recorded Crime Rates and Public Concern about Crime in Glasgow*. Edinburgh: Scottish Office Central Research Unit; Sarno, C., Hough, M. and Bulos, M. (1999) *Developing a Picture of CCTV in Southwark Town Centres: Final Report*. South Bank University Criminal Policy Research Unit; Squires, P. (1998) *CCTV and Crime Reduction in Crawley: An Independent Evaluation of the Crawley CCTV System*. University of Brighton, Health and

Social Policy Research Centre, Faculty of Health, Department of Community Studies; Squires, P. (2000) *CCTV and Crime Reduction in Crawley: Follow-Up Study 2000. An Independent Evaluation of the Crawley CCTV System.* University of Brighton, Health and Social Policy Research Centre.

9   Blixt, M. (1998) 'Kamera på rätt plats kan förebygga brott', APROPÅ *Brottsförebyggande rådets tidsskrift*, 5–6, pp 3–5 (in Swedish.)

10   Phillips, C. (1999) 'A Review of CCTV Evaluations: Crime Reduction Effects and Attitudes Towards Its Use', in Painter and Tilley (1999), op. cit., pp 123–57.

11   Barr, R. and Pease, K. (1990) Crime Placement, Displacement and Deflection, in Tonry, M. and Morris, N. (eds), *Crime and Justice: A Review of Research.* Chicago: University of Chicago Press, Vol. 12, pp 277–318.

12   Eck, J. (1993) The Threat of Crime Displacement, *Criminal Justice Abstracts*, Vol. 25, pp 527–46; Hesseling, R. (1994) 'Displacement: A Review of the Empirical Literature', in Clarke, R.V. (ed.), *Crime Prevention Studies*, Vol. 3. Monsey, NY: Criminal Justice Press, pp 197–230.

13   For a discussion of this issue, see Kuhlhorn, E. (1975) *Deprivation of Freedom and the Police—An Evaluation of the Temporary Custody Act*, Swedish National Council for Crime Prevention, Report No. 4. Stockholm: Liber förlag.

14   Knutsson, J. (1997) Restoring Public Order in a City Park, in Homel, R. (ed.), *Policing for Prevention: Reducing Crime, Public Intoxication and Injury*, Crime Prevention Studies, Vol. 7. Monsey, NY: Criminal Justice Press, pp 133–51.

15   Wilson, J.Q. and Kelling, G. (1982) 'Broken Windows', *Atlantic Monthly*, Vol. 249, No. 3, pp 29–38.

16   Smith, M.J., Clarke, R.V and Pease, K. (2002) Anticipatory Benefits in Crime Prevention, Tilley, N. (ed.), *Analysis for Crime Prevention*, Crime Prevention Studies, Vol. 13. Monsey, NY: Criminal Justice Press, pp 71–88.

17   Yearly average for the two years preceding onset of CCTV. T-tests used for tests of significance.

18   The Mann-Whitney test was used for all tests of significance in this section. For data in Figures 1 and 4 the following scale was used: 'very great problem', 'great problem', 'small problem', 'very small problem' and 'no problem'. In Figures 2 and 4 the following scale was used: 'much worse', 'worse', 'no change', 'better' and 'much better'.

19   Clarke, R.V. (2001) Effective Crime Prevention: Keeping Pace with New Developments, in Chockalingam, K. (ed.), *Forum on Crime and Society.* New York: United Nations Center for International Crime Prevention, Vol. 1, No. 1, pp 27–35; Bennett, T. and Loraine, G. (1996) Public Attitudes Towards CCTV in Public Places, *Studies on Crime and Crime Prevention* (Biannual Review), Vol. 5, No. 1, pp 72–91.

20   Welsh, B.C. and Farrington, D.P. (2002) *Crime Prevention Effects of Closed Circuit Television: A Systematic Review*, Home Office Research Study No. 252. London: Home Office.

Chapter 11

The Potential of Future Image Communications Technology in Crime Prevention

David R. Bull[1]

This chapter pinpoints how future technology may have an impact, looking specifically at emerging video coding and communication technologies. The emergence of advanced communications technology, such as broadband wireless LANs, will facilitate more rapid and flexible deployment of CCTV systems. High-quality coverage will be facilitated by the use of IP networks, both wired and wireless, and backed up by improved video quality and communications perform-ance. Meanwhile data fusion and other techniques will provide improved event analysis of video material. There are opportunities for better crime prevention in the future but they need to be closely monitored and effectively managed.

Introduction

Crime costs the UK economy some £50 billion a year[2] and the security of individuals and their property remains a cause of major public concern. The installation of CCTV (closed circuit television) cameras in commercial premises and high streets, often carried out in partnership with local community schemes, local authorities, police forces and local business, has assisted in detecting crimes such as personal attacks, theft and drug dealing. They also provide benefits in related areas such as public safety, alarm verification and number plate recognition. Recent international terrorist events have also clearly demonstrated the need for video systems capable of maximizing the use of intelligence from both real-time acquisition and post-event analysis.

The impact of imaging and communications technology on detecting and reducing crime has been recognized by a number of national initiatives such as the EPSRC (Engineering and Physical Sciences Research Council) 'Technologies for Crime Prevention and Detection' Programme,[3] which has committed some £7 m to collaborative research in this area. Further examples are given in the recent HMIC (Her Majesty's Inspectorate of Constabularies) report on the evaluation of Special Branches[4] which highlighted the need for a national network for high bandwidth information exchange with interfaces to both mobile and rapidly deployable units. In particular the capture and secure transmission of high-quality multimedia information from multiple sources has been acknowledged as being of paramount importance. The need for a seamless communications infrastructure to facilitate the capture and exchange of secure, reliable and high-quality information, whether in public spaces, private premises or to police officers on the move or at the site of a deployed unit, is also key.

Imaging systems are currently employed in a wide range of crime-related applications. These include:

- personnel screening, luggage, freight and vehicle scanning, explosives detection;

- building security, access control, intruder identification by personal signature;

- public space surveillance for crime detection;

- virtual crime scene construction;

- forensic science (e.g. fingerprint detection);

- person detection/biometrics, visual features, gait, crowd and behavioural analysis;

- vehicle security, traffic analysis, identification and tracking;

- anti-terrorism.

However, concerns still remain over the widespread adoption of this technology. In this context, the questions to be asked of any CCTV or surveillance system are:

- Will the individual image quality be adequate (transmission errors, coding artefacts)?

- What limits resolution—is it the camera, the coding or the recorder?

- Is the frame rate high enough to ensure all activities are adequately captured?

- How might the evidence be tampered with and how can this be prevented and detected?

- Is the transmission secure?

- How does the system perform in low light conditions?

- How is the system affected by viewing variations between daylight and infrared illumination?

- Is the coverage adequate (e.g. camera positions, radio coverage)?

- What degree of back-up storage is available and what is the cost of storage?

- Is the capacity of the system limited—how many cameras can be connected?

- Is the communications infrastructure of sufficient bandwidth and reliability—wired or wireless?

- Solid-state or tape back-up—what happens when the tape runs out?

- What image analysis features are available and desirable—tracking, activity detection, threat assessment?

- Is the control environment and user interface appropriate to the task?

- Is the coding and storage technology compatible with existing standards—is it usable by the police as evidence?

This paper addresses some of these issues in the context of current emerging video coding and communication technologies. The motivation is not to deal in detail with the practical and commercial issues associated with the deployment of existing technology, but rather to argue that these new techniques can lead to improved systems and thus better crime prevention in the future.

Current technology and its limitations

In the past decade we have seen the growth of the Internet and of mobile communications. This success has been due to the rapid development and take-up of digital technology allowing low-cost deployment at reasonable cost to the user. Digital connectivity, coding and storage is rapidly overtaking more established analogue systems in the professional and consumer markets but has made slower penetration in CCTV and surveillance markets. The benefits include:

- *Cost*—digital cameras and data networks are well established in professional and domestic applications. Increased investment and take-up will drive down costs.

- *Reproducibility*—digital information can be copied without distortion. Also tape wear is generally less of an issue with digital storage due to the robustness of the encoding method coupled with advanced error protection techniques.

- *Flexibility*—the potential for adaptation to channel variations in terms of bandwidth (compression) and error performance.

- *Post-processing*—of images and video is possible to facilitate alarm generation and to improve recognition and detection.

- *Standards*—the importance of compatibility for multi-sourcing and media interchange, in particular for evidential purposes.

On the negative side, the issues that have prevented rapid take-up in the CCTV market have included a lack of standards, access to ready-deployed digital communications infrastructure and historical storage and capture costs. In addition, the issue of compatibility between digital storage technologies (e.g. download from integrated hard disk systems) can be a serious issue for police when acquiring evidence.

Electronic surveillance techniques have been classified as belonging to three generations.[5] First generation techniques (1960–1980) employed basic analogue video cameras and transmission techniques, connecting to a control centre for viewing on an array of monitors. Problems arose because of the attention span of operators and the frequent occurrence of missed events, especially in large systems. From around 1980, improvements and cost reductions in sensor, computing and communications technology led to the emergence of more sophisticated processing for event detection, alarm generation, fault detection, illumination compensation and tracking of objects in scenes.[6] Digital transmission techniques also emerged during this so-called second generation and coding standards such as JPEG (still image) and H.261[7] (video) emerged to facilitate basic levels of digital storage and transmission using ISDN lines and solid-state and tape storage. These techniques allowed increased amounts of data to be assimilated due to attention focusing techniques.

From around 2000, a third generation of system began to emerge, exploiting new coding standards, broadband communications and, open protocols, and offering enhanced processing and intelligent sensors.[8] Using Internet and wireless access methods, monitoring is now possible from remote sites. It is also possible to 'fuse' information from different types of sensor in order to offer improved performance. These issues are addressed further in the following sections.

Commercially available CCTV systems are clearly becoming increasingly sophisticated and methods are progressively migrating from the research laboratory into deployed systems.[9] Many now offer specifications similar to those in Table 1.

Table 1. Typical specifications of existing CCTV systems

Frame rate	Sensor/Resolution	Bandwidth/codec[1]	Analysis	Connectivity	Capacity	Authentication
1-25fps	380–580 lines	8Kb/s–2Mb/s	Motion detection	Analogue	10–1000 cameras	Limited
	1/3–1/2 in CCD	MJPEG	Motion trigger	ISDN		Hashing
		H.261	Time lapse	ethernet		
		(H.263)	Illumination compensation	ATM		
			Peak white inversion	IP		
			Tracking and co-operative working			
			(Object recognition (face, number plate))			

[1]The term codec refers to a combined image or video encoder and decoder system.

The challenge of third-generation systems is therefore to provide high-quality data acquisition, efficient and robust coding, high bandwidth and secure transmission, efficient storage with ease of access, and sophisticated processing to allow flexibility of control, adaptation and enhanced event analysis. In particular these systems should offer:

- reduction of reaction time for alert generation, and information-assisted decision-making;

- easy deployment of sensors without large infrastructures, taking advantage of wireless network technologies, with security features for source authentication and content access protection;

- adaptation to the network conditions, which imply the possibilities of scalability for quality of service (QoS) management;

- extraction of metadata from images and video for reporting, indexing and search purposes.

The following sections highlight some existing and emerging technologies which will contribute to these goals.

Camera and coding technologies

Emerging coding standards and H.264

The aim of a digital image or video coding system is to reduce the amount of information required to adequately represent the image or sequence. This is normally achieved through a combination of signal processing (energy compaction), quantization (based on psychovisual criteria) and statistical methods. Despite many years of standards activity in the image and video coding communities, there are currently no common standards for video data storage or transmission in the CCTV industry. Existing digital solutions usually incorporate some form of compression and may also include a proprietary method of encryption or watermarking. Most existing digital CCTV systems are based on intra-frame (i.e. no motion estimation) coding methods such as Motion JPEG.[10] Other approaches have been based on proprietary wavelet coding technology[11]. Motion JPEG-2000 (also based on a wavelet decomposition rather than a discrete cosine transform) is now set to replace M-JPEG. Although M-JPEG 2000 has lower coding efficiency than other video coding schemes discussed in this section, it does offer other benefits in that it provides:

- a natural upgrade path from M-JPEG and proprietary frame-based video coding schemes used in surveillance applications;

- low delay, high resolution (size and bit-depth), robustness to transmission errors, frame-to-frame independence;

- partial access to content using region of interest (RoI) coding;

- the ability to capture high-resolution still images;

- fine-grain scalability which is very useful for adapting the video encoding to the network bandwidth capability;

- security (part 8) and Wireless connectivity (part 11) capabilities.

In order to satisfy the demands of efficient, low-power and low-cost terminal equipment, it will be necessary to adopt more efficient video coding methods. H.263[12,13] was developed between 1995 and 1998 and offered significant improvements over its predecessor, H.261, especially at lower bit rates. This was achieved primarily through the employment of enhanced motion estimation and inherent error resilient modes of operation. Codecs based on H.263 offer substantially improved data compression ratios when compared with JPEG and H.261, therefore requiring reduced bandwidth for transmission or alternatively offering higher quality or frame rate for the same bandwidth.

There has been significant activity in recent years developing video coding techniques which facilitate interactivity and flexible scene compositing. The MPEG-4 standard[14] allows scenes to be decomposed into object planes which can be independently manipulated and combined according to user preferences. This not only provides the basis for a powerful authoring tool, but it may also offer benefits in scene analysis, crime scene reconstruction and region of interest coding. On the negative side, it presents increased complications in image and video authentication (see section 6).

H.264/MPEG-4 part 10 (AVC) is an emerging standard applicable to a wide range of video coding applications including broadcast, consumer, CCTV and surveillance applications. It offers enhanced performance compared to previous standards (up to 50 per cent improvement over H.263 or the MPEG-4 simple profile) by way of new transformation, entropy coding and motion compensation strategies. It also incorporates a range of techniques for loss resilience including slice partitioning and multiple reference frames. The link between H.264 and MPEG-4 will facilitate libraries of common algorithms/tools to be produced which can be used to build sophisticated video-based applications. Finally it offers a conceptual separation between the video coding layer and the network adaptation layer. This can provide improved 'network friendliness', with simpler packetization and better priority control.

Reconfigurable codecs

The rapid growth of and convergence between the computing and communications disciplines has led to the increasing use of reconfigurable and downloadable software for reconfiguration control of terminal hardware. Ultimately this will also lead to the concept of software codecs which might be downloaded either with or prior to the associated content. This offers both greater terminal flexibility and upgradability to the end user. Thus a final system may consist of a higher level language such as Java/MEXE together with a library of common efficient native algorithms or tools. A communications session may start with a negotiation phase to determine the available resources both in terms of hardware, software and networking. Having determined this context information, the system can then negotiate specific content formats and codec type.

The above ideas are important in terms of providing demanding applications which can fully exploit and adapt to environmental and user characteristics. Of particular interest are codecs that can transparently adapt both to user preferences and networking conditions in order to optimize the user's perceived quality of service. In the wider sense, this is likely to imply the use of agents, which can learn the user's preferences and then act on the user's behalf to transparently map this to an optimum choice of system configuration (including codec and network parameters). These agents are likely to reside both within the terminal, the remote terminal and at intervening edge and backbone routers. Such technology may ultimately also impact the design and deployment of CCTV systems.

Error resilient techniques

Error-resilient techniques[15] are becoming increasingly attractive as bearers of multimedia information across noisy environments where packet loss or interference prevails. They can tolerate a certain level of transmission error and provide an acceptable quality of reconstruction without relying solely on forward error correction (FEC) or automatic repeat request (ARQ) methods. In combination with FEC and ARQ, error-resilient techniques can offer improved compression performance in the presence of time-varying bit error rates and are suitable for real-time and multicast applications.

Path diversity and multiple independent data threads[16] have also been proposed as means of establishing reliable video communications in interactive or multicast scenarios where ARQ-based correction is not feasible. Such techniques, while successful, do, however, impose a penalty in terms of bandwidth overhead or quality degradation.

Enhanced error concealment strategies are also important in order to repair corrupted information at the receiver node or control room. This is particularly important in the case of wireless transmission where little or no storage is performed at the camera.[17]

Quality assessment

When measuring image or video quality, several issues have a significant impact:

- compression ratio;

- resolution;

- frame rate;

- error performance;

- system requirements especially for evidential purposes.

Measures of image and video quality should be treated with some caution. Typical objective measures based on mean squared error (MSE) or peak signal to noise ratio (PSNR) assessments simply reflect average distortions across an image and take no account of the impact of the distortion on the human visual system or its localization. Various perceptual studies have been undertaken to assess the impact of losses and distortions in a bitstream, on perceived quality.[18] Clearly the extent of loss temporally and spatially must be considered as well as the local impact and the influence of concealment strategies also needs to be taken into account. It is important that metrics be developed for the objective characterization of codec performance in bandwidth varying and lossy environments.

Subjective assessment methods therefore remain very important and double stimulus (DSCQS)[19] testing as developed for the broadcast industry should be employed against evidential and detection/recognition requirements (standardized as ITU-R.500-6).

Another important factor to be considered is the variation in quality of service for the underlying network. A successful video codec should be able to adapt to environmental and loading variations, providing both resilience to occasional errors or missing data as well as flexibility in varying the source/channel coding trade-offs. All of these factors need to be implemented in a way which offers the user a maximum of flexibility within a simple intuitive user interface.

Efficient and adaptive codec technology

Reliable and sustained information transmission is vital for the types of application envisaged here. Together with optimization of network quality, there is an equivalent need for complementary source encoding and decoding algorithms.

In the case of wireless systems (see section 4), emerging wireless local area networks (WLANs) such as HIPERLAN/2, 802.11a and 802.11g employ a number of physical layer transmission modes with different coding and modulation schemes. These modes are selected by a link adaptation scheme which may use a variety of link-quality measurements like PER (packet error rate), received signal strength, etc. Mode selection is expected to be made according to the quality of service (QoS) required from each user.

Given the level of physical layer adaptation in future communication networks, scalable coding will be essential and will enable terminals with differing capabilities to communicate in a seamless manner. The optimal mapping of physical layer streams for video applications including networking protocol issues/extensions is a key issue. In particular approaches that offer significant potential in fast error recovery, advanced rate control and packet prioritization are of significant interest.

Camera technology

The cost and performance of technology has progressed significantly in recent years. Low-cost, high-performance sensors, embedded codecs and embedded intelligence have all contributed to this. While a full review of camera technology is not possible here, it is worth highlighting two developments. Firstly, high-definition recording technology has, until recently, been solely in the domain of the professional broadcaster and film-maker with equipment costs approaching £100,000 for a single camcorder/VTR combination. There have however, recently been industrial products announced from companies such as Adimec[20] where a camera and lens can be purchased for approximately £10,000. JVC have also recently announced a 720 line (progressive) consumer product which will retail at around £3,000. While still expensive, costs will continue to fall if driven by consumer and industry demand. An issue with this technology is the additional bandwidth required for HD transmission and storage. A key advantage of course is that it need not be operated continuously in high definition mode, but can be triggered according to event analysis.

A second development relates to new sensors such as those from PIXIM[21] which claim pixel-adaptive CMOS sensor technology where each pixel in the image is capable of individual adaptation to lighting conditions. This offers significant potential for high-quality images in mixed or low-light conditions.

Connectivity and deployment

Internet

The Internet has rapidly emerged as a platform for flexible information interchange between individuals and groups. The Internet protocol stack TCP/IP, UDP or RTP also provides a standard means of data collection and exchange in office and more recently CCTV systems. The speed of transmission will vary according to the number of nodes and network loading and can be a dedicated network or part of a wider user network. Existing ADSL access offers up to 2 Mb/s (downlink) corresponding to an increase of up to 40 in terms of data rate compared with V90 modems. Existing deployments often employ 10baseT or 100BaseT ethernet implementations but the emergence of low cost Gigabit Ethernet solutions are likely to have an influence in future high-end systems.

In future CCTV systems, IP systems offer the potential for scaleable, low-cost systems which are location and terminal independent. The potential exists for every camera to offer client and local server capabilities and links to a remote central intelligence server. Each client might integrate different video format encoders and video transport protocols whose behaviour can be dynamically configurable by the local server. A remote central server can then enforce different policies (security, QoS, camera management) to local server modules.

One example of an IP-based CCTV system is the Baxall Destiny IP range[22] employing technolgy form IndigoVision. Such a system has, for example, recently been installed in Brussels Airport. This is based on an existing ethernet infrastructure and incorporates over 600 cameras covering baggage handling, customs, security check-in and retail.

Activities under the Internet2 initiative coupled with high bandwidth infrastructures will enhance capabilities still further in the coming years.

Wireless cellular and WLAN systems
Hanzo et al. offer some insight into the future of interactive cellular video telephony[23] and the topic is also covered in depth by Bull et al.[24]

Second-generation (2 G and 2.5 G) cellular systems such as GSM and GPRS offer relatively low data rates up to 64 kb/s, and are generally considered to be inappropriate for most CCTV type applications. Third-generation cellular systems also currently only offer 64 kb/s although this is likely to rise to 384 kb/s in the medium term. Competition in this field also comes from 2.5 G technologies such as EDGE (Enhanced Data-rate GSM Evolution). Although some manufacturers have exploited these technologies (Pedagog's OCTV system for example[25]), the available bit-rates severely limit frame-rate, resolution and/or quality. Even with future 3 G technology, sustained high-throughput data from large numbers of cameras in a restricted area is likely to overload a network unless hot-spot technology is utilized. Therefore, in the short to medium term, greater potential is possible from wireless local area networks (WLANs).

WLAN boards such as those based on the IEEE 802.11b standard offer up to 11 Mb/s for a modest price (less than US$100). Various wireless technologies are, however, emerging which will enable range and data rate to be increased still further. WLANs such as IEEE802.11a, HIPERLAN/2, 802.11e and 802.11g offer raw data rates in excess of 50 Mb/s, while future systems promise bit-rates well in excess of 100 Mb/s. Such systems will provide the primary focus for emerging third-generation hot-spots in office and domestic LANs as they offer flexible physical layer transmission, with the mode of operation being selected by a link-adaptation scheme. Delay sensitive applications such as voice or video transmissions demand more complex link adaptation algorithms that provide better QoS. These must optimize throughput while complying with latency constraints.

The emergence of higher bandwidth standards will move us toward 4 G systems. These will no doubt be based on multiple input, multiple output (MIMO) technology and employ sectorized antennas. As well as offering capacity enhancements, these standards will be exploited to employ spatial multiplexing as a means of relaying and ad hoc networking.

Wireless network planning for rapid deployment
The optimum deployment of WLANs in a highly constrained environment is a complex task that involves the choice of radio standard, optimum site locations, antenna structure, power level and operating frequency. Algorithms are currently being researched that will simplify the design and construction of a high-quality video surveillance network. The University of Bristol has previously developed a number of cellular radio optimization modules. These allow the WLAN to be dimensioned using user-supplied coverage and capacity data together with information on potential access point and wireless router locations (building roof or corner locations, lamp-posts, etc).

The relaying of data between terminals and the performance of the wireless router critically depends on the propagation conditions. Path loss, fast fading and temporal and spatial correlation for an outdoor mounted access point and for mobile terminal to mobile terminal channels all have significant impact.

The combination of broadband wireless LAN technology with accurate environmental prediction and planning tools will no doubt enable the rapid and optimized deployment of wireless camera technology in the future.

Quality of service management
Integrated algorithms will be required in future systems that are able to adapt information quality and quantity according to various constraints. This middleware must be aware of network topology and make decisions to adapt information flows in accordance with QoS service requirements.

QoS adaptation depends for example on a range of factors:

• constraints linked to transport layers;

• bandwidth availability and congestion;

- error environment;

- end user terminal profile (PC, PDA, pocket PC);

- content protection and content access rights.

One of the potential benefits of 3 G UMTS is its enhanced IP mobility management and its QoS control capabilities. UMTS defines a range of QoS levels that are appropriate for real-time video communication together with interactive modes which facilitate web access or video database search.

Image analysis technology

Although video surveillance has been shown to offer significant benefits in crime prevention and detection there is still a requirement for further automation to allow improved tracking, object recognition, alarm generation and intelligent retrieval. This section outlines some of the ways in which these can be achieved.

Automatic detection of events through image content analysis
Image segmentation, analysis and enhancement techniques have been re-searched for many years and have found application in military, industrial and forensic applications. These range from relatively simple algorithms for motion detection (for example to trigger an alarm, start recording or detect the early signs of smoke and heat haze) to much more complex tracking and modelling methods. Recording to tape or disk can also be activated by conventional passive infrared motion detectors. More advanced techniques have been employed to track a targeted object (person/face/car) across a scene, even through a crowd, and automatically hand over to the next camera in a CCTV surveillance network. Such techniques suffer when occlusions occur in a scene. However several authors (e.g. Dockstader et al.) have developed a means of tracking multiple humans in the presence of occlusions by combining views from multiple cameras.[26]

Multimedia search and retrieval
As amounts of data acquired and archived from CCTV systems increases, there is a growing need to employ advanced asset management systems, including methods to allow automatic labelling, metadata extraction and intelligent content based retrieval. Smart access to content is required using advanced search and indexing tools similar to those used for text queries currently on the Internet. This has been an active research field for several years.[27] Content describing tools such as MPEG-7[28] will gain increasing importance, especially for police and evidential work. It is of course essential that standards are adopted to ensure compatibility between systems. MPEG-7 standardizes structures and languages for search and query, but it does not

standardize how features are extracted from a scene or clip. Examples of low-level or primitive features include colour, shape, texture, motion and location. In order to extract meaning from a scene, these need to be combined into semantic features such as actions, events, people and places. This is the topic of extensive ongoing research.

Biometrics
Vision techniques to automatically analyse image sequences from videos to detect criminal intention, suspicious behaviour and criminal actions are much more difficult. Behaviour can be modelled using psychophysical techniques to identify precise information in complex scenes. Detecting and tracking individual humans in video sequences is, however, a difficult problem. Active Shape Models can be employed to detect and track whole body motion, in conjunction with more localized techniques, like spatial, colour, texture and region analysis, to detect and track body parts.

A number of projects have attempted reliably to extract meaningful information from a video in real time about malicious intent, suspicious or criminal behaviour and dangerous situations. For example, a joint project between Leeds and Reading Universities is working on combining techniques for tracking vehicles with that of identifying 'suspicious' behaviour of pedestrians.

It is extremely difficult to automatically recognize faces, even in a controlled environment. CCTV systems, especially those viewing public spaces, are by definition unconstrained. However, software has been developed by Visionics which forms the basis for the Mandrake system, which, it is claimed, can recognize faces in a crowd in real-time. Mandrake is already installed at football stadia, and has been linked to the London Borough of Newham's street camera network with limited success.

Multisensor surveillance, fusion and virtual viewpoint synthesis
Networks of video cameras operating in a cooperative fashion have been proposed to facilitate enhanced performance. This approach has been adopted by the DARPA Video Surveillance and Monitoring (VSAM) project[29] where objects are not only tracked but their positions in 3-D space are also identified.

In rapidly deployable multimedia networks, it is inevitable that camera positions will be heavily constrained and that coverage will be limited and often sparse. In certain circumstances it will be possible to enhance visualization through view interpolation and synthesis to offer a pseudo look-around capability to enhance detection. This will also facilitate geometrical analysis of a scene for threat assessment or post-event analysis. However, several hard research problems need to be addressed before this can be successful. For example, problems exist due to effects such as photometric variations and texture-less image regions. Complexity is also a key issue as is determining the optimum weighting function for interpolation. This will be influenced by the shape of the objects within the scene. A further issue, especially in arbitrarily deployed cameras, is that of occlusion. This worsens with the sparseness of array. Without taking into account the 3-D geometry of the overall scene, it is not possible to correctly determine the position of occlusions. Taking advantage of the geometry between pairs of images allows the search for correspondences to be simplified.

The relative positions of each of the cameras will have an impact on the computational complexity and accuracy of any 'virtual camera' technique, and on the type of geometric simplifications that can be applied. A method to determine the optimal set of reference views is therefore required and this is a challenge for future research.

Image and video authentication

Concerns have been raised by the police and the legal profession over the authenticity and hence admissibility of digitally stored video and images as evidence. A recent report by the House of Lords has addressed this issue.[30] Even using inexpensive software packages, sophisticated alterations to digital images can easily be performed and are often difficult to detect by eye. Such modifications might be used for benefit, for example to provide enhancements for improved identification and detection, or might be malicious, for example by a CCTV system owner wishing to create false evidence, or even by the police.

The report indicates that the existence of such technology need in itself be of no great concern, but that caution must be taken when using and judging such evidence. The report concludes by stating: 'We support the application of any technology which can help with the verification of an image and provide assistance to the court in assessing its worth.' The weight of such evidence will therefore be determined by the confidence in it. Authentication methods such as encryption or watermarking alongside a secure audit trail (from initial image to copy) are therefore vital in raising this confidence.

In response to this report, the Home Office PSDB in association with the Association of Chief Police Officers (ACPO) have prepared a Digital Imaging Procedure for Handling Evidence.[31]

There has been a significant amount of interest in recent years in the area of digital watermarking to provide inherent authentication capabilities for images and video. In particular, so-called fragile watermarks are important as these are designed to change when an image has been tampered with. Potential benefits of fragile watermarks over competing techniques include:

- The watermark is invisible to a human observer.

- The watermark is altered by the application of common signal processing techniques.

- It is difficult for an unauthorized person to insert a false watermark.

- The watermark can quickly be extracted by an authorized person.

- The areas where any tampering took place can be determined.

- It is possible to characterize the nature of the attack, differentiate between legal and illegal attacks, and possibly reconstruct the image.

- It should be possible to insert the watermark in the compressed domain.[32]

The purpose of fragile watermarks is to detect whether an image has been tampered with since the watermark was inserted. A fragile watermark should be destroyed by the changes to the image. Obviously, there are certain types of operation that may be considered 'legal' depending on the application. These include cropping, resizing, colour enhancement and lossy compression.

Inevitably, there are a vast number of different ways that a watermark can be inserted into an image. One of the most important distinctions is in what domain the watermark is inserted. Early techniques employed the spatial domain, whereas later methods used the discrete cosine transform (DCT)[33] and wavelet transform[34] domains. Indeed, the fact that there is no standardized approach to this presents major issues in compatibility.

Provided that changes in images can be detected, the next challenge is to estimate what tampering has taken place, and to then correct it.[35,36] Although it is not possible to perfectly reconstruct the image, it may be possible to determine an estimate of the original image.

Conclusions

Technology has already had a major impact on detecting and reducing crime. In the future, technology can continue to contribute by providing new means of support for flexible acquisition, intelligent manipulation and broadband communication of high-quality video data. This will be achieved through advanced camera technology, new coding techniques and sophisticated image processing. In addition, the emergence of advanced communications technology including broadband wireless LANs will facilitate more rapid and flexible deployment.

In summary, this paper has proposed that the benefits of future systems could include:

- rapid active and reactive network deployment through the use of advanced radio propagation analysis and planning tools;

- new wireless local area network (WLAN) architectures including base stations and ad hoc relaying taking into account the requirements for both mobile cameras and optimized fixed camera locations;

- efficient, high-quality, robust and scalable video coding schemes appropriate for delivery to and from fixed or mobile terminals;

- maximized intelligence through the fusion of multiple video sources for enhanced detection, tracking and arbitrary viewpoint synthesis.

Coverage to multiple fixed and mobile cameras at the required quality will be enabled through the use of IP networks operating in both wired and wireless environments. Enhanced performance will be obtained through optimization of both video (view) quality and communication system performance during network deployment. Finally, post- and during-event analysis of video material will offer improved visualization and tracking through the use of data fusion and arbitrary viewpoint synthesis techniques. These, alongside other techniques, will assist in maximizing the utility of surveillance information leading to improved operations management.

Notes

1   Professor David Bull is a founder and currently Chairman of ProVision Communication Technologies Ltd, a wireless multimedia spin-off from the University of Bristol. He is also Professor of Signal Processing at the University of Bristol and Head of the Electrical and Electronic Engineering Department where he leads the Signal Processing Research Group; email Dave.Bull@ bristol.ac.uk. He has worked widely in signal processing with recent research focusing on the problems of image and video communications (in particular error resilient source coding, linear and non-linear filterbanks, scalable methods, content based coding and architectural optimization). He has published over 250 papers and 2 books in these areas and has been awarded two IEE Premiums. He has also been a director of the VCE in Digital Broadcasting and Multimedia Technology and a member of the UK Foresight ITEC panel. He is currently a member of the Science and Technology Board for the UK MOD Defence Technology Centre in Data and Information Fusion and of the DTI funded research Centre – 3CRL.

2   Simmons, J. (2002) *Crime in England and Wales 2001/2002*, ~~~ ~~~ ment and Statistics, Home Office, July.

3   *http://epsrc.ac.uk/crime/*.

4   Blakey, D. (2003) *A Need to F* *and Ports Policing*, Home C

5   Peterson, J. (2001) *Understanding Surveillance Techniques*. Florida: CRC Press.

6   Foresti, G.L. (1998) Object Detection and Tracking in Time Varying and Badly Illuminated Outdoor Environments, *SPIE Journal of Optical Engineering*, Vol. 37, No. 9, pp 2550–64.

7   ITU-T Recommendation H.261: Video Codec for Audiovisual Services at px64kb/s, version 2, March 1993.

8   Special Edition on Third Generation Surveillance Systems, *Proc. IEEE*, 89 (2001).

9   Pavlidis, I., Morellas, V., Tsiamyrtzis, P. and Harp, S. (2001) Urban Surveillance Systems: From the Laboratory to the Commercial World, *Proc. IEEE*, Vol. 89, No. 10, pp 1478–97.

10   ISO/IEC 10918-1/ITU-T Recommendation T.81, Digital Compression and Coding of Continuous Tone Still Images, 1992.

11   *http://pedagog.com/*.

12   ITU-T Recommendation H.263: Video Coding for Low Bit-rate Communications, version 1998.

13   Al-Mualla, M., Canagarajah, C., Bull, D. (2002) *Video Coding for Mobile Applications*. Florida: Academic Press.

14   Puri, A, and Eleftheriadis, A. (1998) 'MPEG-4: An Object Based Multimedia Coding Standard Supporting Mobile Applications', *ACM Journal on Mobile Networks and Applications*, Vol. 3, pp 5–32.

15   Sadka, A. (2002) *Compressed Video Communication*. Chichester: Wiley.

16   Goyal, V.K. (2001) Multiple Description Coding: Compression meets the Network, *IEEE Signal Processing Magazine*, September, pp 74–93.

17   Sadka, op. cit.

18   Netravali, A.N. and Haskell, B. (1995) *Digital Pictures*, 2nd edn. New York: Plenum Press.

19   Ibid.

20   *http://adimec.com*.

21   *http://pixim.com/*.

22   *http://baxall.com/*.

23   Hanzo, I., Cherriman, P. and Kuan, E. (2000) Interactive Cellular and Cordless Video Telephony: State of the Art, Design Principles and Expected Performances, *Proc. IEEE*, Vol. 88, No. 5, pp 611–42.

24   Bull, D., Canagarajah, C. and Nix, A., (1999) *Insights into Mobile Multimedia Communication*. Florida: Academic Press.

        ://pedagog.com/.

        S. and Tekalp, M. (2001) 'Multiple Camera Tracking of Interacting Motion', *Proc. IEEE*, Vol. 89, No. 10, pp 1441–55.

27 Chang, S., Huang, Q., Puri, A., Shaharay, B. and Huang, T. (2000) Multimedia Search and Retrieval, in Ouri, A. and Chen, T. (eds), *Multimedia Systems and Networks*. New York: Marcel Dekker.

28 ISO/IEC JTC1/SC29/WG11 N4031, Overview of the MPEG-7 Standard, March 2001.

29 Collins, R., Lipton, A., Fujiyoshi, H. and Kanade, T. (2001) Algorithms for Cooperative Multisensor Surveillance, *Proc. IEEE*, Vol. 89, No. 10, pp 1456–77.

30 Digital Images as Evidence, House of Lords, session 1997–98, 5th report, Select Committee on Science and Technology, HL paper 64, HMSO.

31 Home Office PSDB, Digital Imaging Procedure version 1.0: Guidance on Handling Digital Images as Evidence, March 2002, PSDB publication February 02.

32 Lin, E.T. and Delp, E.J. (1999) A Review of Fragile Image Watermarks, *Proc. of the Multimedia and Security Workshop* (ACM Multimedia '99), Orlando, FL, pp 25–9.

33 Wu, M. and Liu, B. (1998) 'Watermarking for Image Authentication', *Proc. ICIP 1998*. IEEE International Conference on Image Processing, Vol. 2, pp 399–403.

34 Kundur, D. and Hatzinakos, D. (1999) Digital Watermarking for Telltale Tamper Proofing and Authentication, *Proc. IEEE*, Vol. 87, No. 7, pp 1167–80.

35 Fridich, J. and Goljan, M. (1999) 'Images with Self-Correcting Capabilities, *Proc. ICIP 1999*, Kobe, Japan, October.

36 Knowles, H., Winne, D., Canagrajah, C. and Bull, D. On the Use of Robust Watermarks for Tamper Detection, submitted to *IEEE Trans. Image Processing* (copy available from author).

Index

Crime Prevention and Community Safety:
An International Journal

Perpetuity Training

Perpetuity Training specialises in the field of crime, security and risk management. Our training courses have been designed for managers and practitioners in these fields and are suitable for both UK and overseas clients. Areas of study include:

Security & Risk Management
The Prevention & Management of Violence
Law & Security
Information Technology
Business Skills & Management Procedures

In designing and developing the course content we take account of leading research in each area and combine this with good practice both in the UK and abroad. All of our courses are delivered by experts and designed to enable you to produce the best possible solution for your particular needs.

How to Evaluate the Effectiveness of CCTV

This course will guide you through the process of designing and conducting an evaluation of your CCTV system. The course will equip you with the knowledge and skills to determine if your system is working to its full potential or not, and whether it is providing you with a good return on your investment. The course will cover:

* What an evaluation is designed to achieve
* Understanding evaluation methods
* What can be learned about the way the programme was implemented
* How to measure the programme impact
* How to measure cost effectiveness
* How to conduct a cost benefit analysis
* How to learn from the results of an evaluation

Perpetuity Conferences

Perpetuity Conferences run and organise conferences, seminars and workshops in the fields of security, risk and crime prevention. Our conferences are based upon the very latest research and best practice, with information and advice from leading industry experts. Conferences include:

Is CCTV Working?
Are public perceptions of CCTV realistic? What do offenders think of CCTV? Does CCTV displace crime?

Retail Crime: What are the Solutions?
How do offenders commit credit card fraud? What do shoplifters think of security? Does CCTV work in retailing?

Information for both training courses and conferences, and on-line booking, is also available on our website:

www.perpetuitygroup.com

Alternatively please contact Perpetuity Conferences Ltd or Perpetuity Training Ltd at:

Perpetuity Group
50 Queens Road, Leicester, LE2 1TU, UK
Tel: +44 (0) 116 221 7777; Fax: +44 (0) 116 221 7171

Email: training@perpetuitygroup.com / conferences@perpetuitygroup.com

.